T
VISITOF
OF TEXTS

THE
VISITOR'S BOOK
OF TEXTS

OR

THE WORD BROUGHT NEAR

TO

THE SICK AND SORROWFUL

Andrew A. Bonar

THE BANNER OF TRUTH TRUST

THE BANNER OF TRUTH TRUST
3 Murrayfield Road, Edinburgh EH12 6EL, UK
P.O. Box 621, Carlisle, PA 17013, USA

ISBN: 978 1 84871 071 9

Typeset in 10/15 pt Sabon at
the Banner of Truth Trust

Printed in the U.S.A. by
Versa Press, Inc.,
East Peoria, IL

All Scripture quotations, unless otherwise stated
are taken from the Authorised Version.

The text has been lightly edited by the publishers
for this new edition.

CONTENTS

PART II

THE WORD BROUGHT NEAR TO SEVEN CLASSES WHO MAY BE FOUND IN THE SICK ROOM

PART III

THE WORD BROUGHT NEAR TO THE SORROWFUL

Introduction

Wchat we *say* to the sick should be brief: and when we *pray* with the sick we should be short in our prayers. One who for some weeks lay within the shadow of eternity, though afterwards restored, writes, 'Few things are more injurious than very long prayers at sick-beds. I am persuaded that short, frequent, and, I may add, fervent prayers at a sick-bed, are most suitable.' He says again, 'I am persuaded that those that visit the sick would do well to confine themselves to the simplest view of Scripture truth; and it may be well, also, that these views should be embodied in some select texts of Scripture. It was in this way that Dr C. treated me when I was under those fears, and I have admired his wisdom. He approached my bedside, and after hearing my views, he repeated the text, "This is the record, that God has given us eternal life; and this life is in his Son." He again repeated it until he saw that I held it in my mind.' He adds, that when other mental strength failed him, *'The exercise of faith in the Saviour never fatigued him. Like the hand, it retains its grasp firm in death.'*—*Thoughts in the Prospect of Death.*

This book is formed upon this principle; for the testimony quoted is not a solitary case. Indeed, it originated in the feeling of two Christian friends, that something which would help a visitor to deal thus with the sick was most desirable. A Book of Texts, while it may furnish ready materials to some, will lead on others to passages of a like kind which are not given, and which the visitor may feel to be all the more interesting and fresh, because he has himself lighted on them, without the help of foreign suggestion.

The same principle applies to our dealing with the Sorrowful to a considerable extent. When we succeed in arresting their thoughts so as to fix them on one single text, we have not laboured in vain for their comfort. One text sunk in the mighty waters of their sorrow may be an anchor dropped. It was this that Cecil sought when he was watching with intense anxiety over a friend; 'All I can do is to go from text to text like a bird from spray to spray.' Many, however, from long experience in such cases, have found it good occasionally to do a little more, though still with the help of a text or portion of the Word. And at times they have found it useful to ask the sick or the sorrowful to ponder the text left with them, after their visitor is gone; and they speak of it at the next visit. The effect of your suggesting that possibly at next visit it may be referred to is this, the person keeps it in memory, and feels interested in it more than would otherwise have been the case.

The Lord himself occasionally deals in this direct textual way, if we may so call it. In an 'Address from a Pastor to his People' (remarkable for its simplicity and solemnity), by the late Dr Brewster of Craig, there is an instance of what we speak of.

> On the day when my bodily life seemed to be at its lowest ebb, and when it was thought by those around me that I could not see another day on earth, I passed through a singular exercise of mind . . . This exercise consisted in a succession of Scripture passages, which I was not conscious of seeking, but which darted as it were into my mind in a moment, and which seemed to require my assent to their truth, and my willingness to testify to their power. These passages seemed to me at the time to come forward in so suitable an order and connection, that I remember of wishing that I could recollect them aright, if I should live to record them . . . This exercise continued a long time, and consisted of two distinct portions. The *first* seemed to be designed to show me the only sure ground of hope to sinful man, and the glory of God's sovereign grace in the salvation of sinners. The passages were such as these: 'Come now and let us reason together, saith the Lord, though your sins be as scarlet, they shall be as white as snow, though they be red like crimson, they shall be as wool.' 'To this man will I look, even to him that is poor and of a contrite spirit,

and trembleth at my word.' 'God was in Christ reconciling the world to himself, not imputing their trespasses unto them.' 'For God so loved the world, that he gave his only begotten Son, that whosoever believeth in him should not perish, but have everlasting life.' 'Come unto me, all ye that labour and are heavy laden, and I will give you rest.' 'Let him that is athirst come. And whosoever will, let him take the water of life freely.' 'Behold, I stand at the door, and knock: if any man hear my voice, and open the door, I will come in to him, and will sup with him, and he with me.' 'Unto him that loved us, and washed us from our sins in his own blood, And hath made us kings and priests unto God and his Father; to him be glory and dominion for ever and ever. Amen.'

The *second* portion of this exercise of mind, through which I passed close upon the former, seemed to be designed to show the excellency of the knowledge of Christ, through whom we receive forgiveness of sins, and have peace with God by faith in his name; and to make me feel my obligation (if again sent forth as a preacher of the gospel), to testify such precious truths in face of all revilings, threatenings, and persecutions; to do this, if needful, in the humblest and most toilsome manner, by the highways and hedges; in the streets and lanes of the cities—to do this by teaching from house to house, warning every man, night and day, with tears—labouring among the poorest lambs of the flock, passing, if called, to dark heathen lands, and in the midst of the most savage tribes of men, willing to suffer all things, and to lose all things, and to lay down life itself in thus serving Christ, and seeking to win souls to his glory. All this was done in the same way as before, by words of Scripture darting into my mind and demanding my assent. They were such as these, . . .

Introduction

We do not continue our extract. We have gained what we wished in showing, by means of what has been said, how the Lord himself dealt with a beloved servant of his, who saw in his latter days a blessed work of revival in his flock. We have seen that in the time of both sorrow and sickness, texts from the written Word were plentifully given to this suffering servant, as crumbs from the Master's table, or rather to be to him like Elijah's cake baked on the coals, and cruse of water, strengthening him for a journey to the mount of God (*1 Kings* 19:6). If it is the Lord's way thus to use his Word, the stewards of the household will no doubt be taught by him to select the food needed by various members of the household. One such text as those mentioned above, or one such as this guide book might suggest to visitors of the sick or sorrowful, may be effectual for doctrine, for reproof, for correction, for instruction in righteousness, for consolation, for exhortation, for building up, if only the Holy Ghost breathe it on the soul from the lips of the speaker. When Bengel was dying, a student of the Institution over which he presided called to inquire for him. Bengel requested from him a word of comfort before he left. The young student, abashed and confused, said, that he did not know how to speak to one so learned; but at last contrived to utter the text, 'The blood of Jesus Christ, his Son, cleanseth us from all sin.' 'That is the very word I want', said Bengel; 'it is quite enough!'

Of course it is with the prayer that the Spirit of truth the Comforter, may apply the words spoken, that any portion must be handled, whether by minister or elder, by visitor or friend. For 'God giveth the increase.' 'When he giveth quietness, who then can make trouble? and when he hideth his face, who then can behold him?' (*Job* 36:29).

Should any wish to have a sample of works that may be consulted with great profit by those who deal with the sick and sorrowful, we suggest, out of a vast variety—

Adams' *Private Thoughts*.

Arden's *Scripture Abbreviates*.

Baxter's *Christian Economics*.

Bayley's *Practice of Piety*.

Bonar's *Night of Weeping*.

Boston's *Crook in the Lot*.

Brooks' *Mute Christian*.

Buchanan on *Affliction*.

Case's *Mount Pisgah*.

Cecil's *Visit to the House of Mourning*; and on *Visiting Death-beds*.

Clark's *Promises*.

Flavel's *Token for Mourners*.

Grosvenor's *Mourner*; or, *The Afflicted Relieved*

Hawkes' *Life*.

Hill's *It is well,* or *The Shunamite*.

Introduction

Hymns for the Sick Chamber—larger type.[1]

Janeway's *Life; Invisible Realities.*

Memorial of Two Sisters.

Pearce's *Voice in Rama Hushed.*

Pitcairn's *Perfect Peace.*

Rintoul's *Thoughts on the Prospect of Death.*

Rutherford's *Letters.*

Sibbes' *Bruised Reed.*

Swinnock's *Christian Man's Calling.*

Tweedie's *Balm from Gilead.*

Willison's *Afflicted Man' Companion.*

Zachary Boyd's *Last Battle of the Soul.*

As for such well-meant treatises as those of Hickes, Spincke, Paley, and Stonehouse, as well as the better known work of Jeremy Taylor, *Holy Living and Dying,* they are defective in gospel truth. A sinner might be led to Sinai by them, but could scarcely find his way to Calvary. They leave the impression that while all salvation-work has been wrought by Christ, we *must earn a title to the application of that work* by a process of laborious effort, by long waiting, or by some such previous qualification. It is not so with the other writers named above. They proclaim the tidings that it is the sinner's *first duty,* as well as *privilege,* to 'see the Son and believe upon him', and so

---

[1] All *Taylor's large type series of works* might be recommended for the use of the sick themselves.

have eternal life. In that very rich, but quaint old book by Zachary Boyd, *The Last Battle of the Soul in Death,* he says to the sick and dying:

> My counsel is, that above all things ye have recourse unto the bloody wounds of Christ, wherein, as in the holes of the rock, your soul, like a dove, may find a place of refuge. His wounds well may I call, 'The secret of the Most High'; he who lodgeth there is under the shadow of the Almighty.

PART I

THE WORD BROUGHT NEAR TO THE SICK

'But as for me, when they were sick, my clothing was sackcloth: I humbled my soul with fasting; and my prayer returned into mine own bosom. I behaved myself as though he had been my friend or brother: I bowed down heavily, as one that mourneth for his mother' (*Psa.* 35:13-14, the words of the Lord Jesus).

'And whosoever shall give to drink unto one of these little ones a cup of cold water only in the name of a disciple, verily I say unto you, he shall in no wise lose his reward' (*Matt.* 10:42).

INTRODUCTION TO CHAPTER 1

THE BELIEVER IS SICK

1. Let me call to mind—It is the Lord's will that I should visit the sick. Think of Heb. 13:3; Jas. 5:14; Matt. 25:36. Jesus himself used to do so—John 11:1, 3. Let me then go, saying, 'Lord, send me', for it is as if he were asking, 'Whom shall I send?' (*Isa.* 6:8).

2. I need his presence with me—Exod. 33:14, 15. And so my prayer ascends for 'the Comforter, the Spirit of truth, that he may testify of Christ' (*John* 15:26). Lord Jesus, give me the tongue of the learned, that I may know to speak a word in season to him that is weary (*Isa.* 50:4). Lord, open thou my lips.

3. Let me remember the awful sin of 'healing slightly' the hurt of any. This is marked as one of the greatest of all sins in those who teach. See Jer. 6:14; 8:11; Ezek. 13:10, 16; Lam. 2:14.

Armed with such thoughts, I seek to ascertain on solid ground (not taking it for granted, not even though most others think so), that the person is a believer. If he is so, then perhaps I take such a text as Psa. 40:17, 'I am poor and needy, yet the Lord thinketh upon me.' I repeat it to the sick. Perhaps, I exhibit it as holding up before his eyes a picture of himself, poor and needy in soul and in bodily frame, full of weakness, the body's state a type of the soul's. Then I hold up to view the Lord full of might and mercy; 'The Lord thinketh upon me', as Stephen under the shower of stones was thought upon as by 'the Son of man at the right hand of God.' I try to leave very specially this impression, that the thoughts of our God to us in Christ are thoughts of peace and not of evil—manifold mercy to us the guilty. And then I pray, not in many words, but holding up fully the case of the believing one, and seeking to do so fervently and cordially, like the friends, Mark 1:80, telling of the sick, and inviting the Mighty One's aid.

I

THE BELIEVER IS SICK

John 18:11. 'The cup which my Father hath given me, shall I not drink it?'

> 1. Christ held to his lips the cup of wrath for sin, and drank it to the dregs. The Father was well pleased with his suffering unto death. This is your *atonement*. There is not in the universe one grain of atonement elsewhere. 2. Christ had regard to the Father's will in all he suffered. He took the cup out of the Father's hand, finding this looking to the Father his only relief under all he bore. He is your *Example*.

Psa. 40:17. 'But I am poor and needy! yet the Lord thinketh on me.'

Psa. 36:4-6. 'I sought the Lord, and he heard me, and delivered me from all my fears. They looked unto him and were lightened . . . This poor man cried, and the Lord heard.'

> 1. The believer cries, and at the same time *looks*; for he

5

is heard because of the Saviour to whom he looks. 2. He is not heard because of his cries, nor yet because he is a believer who cries, but because of *him in whom he believes* while he cries.

Psa. 121:1-2. 'I will lift up mine eyes unto the hills, from whence cometh my help. My help cometh from the Lord.'

Psa. 130:5. 'I wait for the Lord, my soul doth wait, and in his word do I hope.'

1. Like Jacob waiting to see God reveal his full salvation. 2. Resting upon the true and faithful sayings of God, not upon anything of a personal kind, such as character, experience, knowledge, services.

John 11:3. 'Therefore his sisters sent unto him, saying, Lord, behold, he whom thou lovest is sick.'

John 13:1. 'When Jesus knew that his hour was come, that he should go out of this world unto the Father, having loved his own which were in the world, he loved them to the end.'

Christ is *your soul's resting-place*. His love flows to your guilty soul in his shed blood, which is freely given to you; and he manifested that love to the very last hour he was with his disciples. In his agony now beginning, he thought of his own more than ever. Bathe your soul in this unchanging love. Our love to him is a stream ever ready to run dry; his love to us is a full tide, and a tide that knows no ebb.

Isa. 40:28-29. 'Hast thou not known, hast thou not heard, that the everlasting God, the Lord, the Creator of the ends of the earth, fainteth not, neither is weary? He giveth power to the faint; and to them that have no might he increaseth strength.'

Isa. 63:9. 'In all their affliction he was afflicted, and the Angel of his Presence saved them: in his love and in his pity he redeemed them; and he bare them, and carried them all the days of old.'

> Here is, 1. Sympathy in the heart of his Father; 2. Salvation by the Saviour who redeemed Israel from the house of bondage; 3. Careful preservation, as when a parent is carrying his tender child over flinty ground.

Matt. 25:36, 40. 'I was sick . . . Inasmuch as ye have done it to the least of these my brethren.'

> Christ has identified himself with his own, in their sick-chamber as much as in their prisons.

Jer. 3125. 'I have satiated the weary soul, I have replenished every sorrowful soul.'

> This is the God with whom you have to do; the God who will wash Israel's bleeding feet; who will pardon Jerusalem-sinners; who will turn forgiven Israel's sorrow into joy, and sanctify them by all their tribulations; who will take down their harps from the willows.

Mal. 3:17. 'I will spare them as a man spareth his own son that serveth him.'

In the day of wrath that comes on other men, the Lord spares his Noahs and his Lots. Their afflictions also are made light, for his heart yearns over his children.

Isa. 27:8. 'In measure when it shooteth forth [*i.e.* when the rod of chastisement is put forth], thou wilt debate with it: he stayeth his rough wind in the day of the east wind.'

2 Tim. 2:1. 'Thou, therefore, my son, be strong in the grace that is in Christ Jesus.'

Thy strength lies in knowing and believing the free love of Jesus to the guilty, and in ever resorting to it. He tells thee that he knows that 'the spirit indeed is willing, but the flesh is weak', Matt. 26:41. How precious is his grace!

Heb. 3:14. 'We are made partakers of Christ, if we hold the beginning of our confidence stedfast unto the end.'

1. Your confidence toward God began in your believing the record that God has given us concerning his Son. It was not founded on your own merit, nor on your being one whit better than other men, nor upon your religious services, nor upon your prayers. It rested wholly on the Father having accepted Christ in your room. 2. As, then, you were accepted when you first of all came to the mercy-seat without regard to one single action of yours; so it must be still, after a life of service. You stood, on the first day you came to the Holy God, and said, 'I deserve an everlasting hell, if looked at in myself, but I claim an everlasting heaven, while I point to the Lord Jesus.' 3. Hold fast this foundation truth with which you began. Hold it fast in your dying hour. Cast not your eye on aught else.

Flee from good deeds and bad deeds alike, in this matter; flee to him who cried, 'It is finished.'

John 6:29. 'This is the work of God [*q.d.* call it *work* if you will, but this is all God asks of you], that ye believe in him whom he hath sent.'

Jude 21. 'Keep yourselves in the love of God, looking for the mercy of the Lord Jesus Christ unto eternal life.'

Keep in the sunshine of God's love to you; this is the sure way to keep your own heart loving God. Dwell in this palace, built up of God's great love to us; and from its windows look out for those discoveries of mercy which the day of Christ shall bring, when he gives you the crown of life with 'mercy' inscribed on it.

John 14:1. 'Let not your heart be troubled'; and verse 27, 'Peace I leave with you, my peace I give unto you; not as the world giveth give I unto you. Let not your heart be troubled, neither let it be afraid.'

1. This chapter is only for *believers*, for it is only Christ's peace that quells fear. 2. The *fearful* are the *faithless* (*Mark* 4:40); for Christ believed in casts out fear.

Exod. 15:26. 'I am the Lord that healeth thee.'

1. He proclaimed himself Physician of the camp of Israel, keeping off disease, or relieving under it. He has been incarnate since then, but has the same power. 2. If then my disease is at his disposal, no doubt he has selected it and fixed its time.[1]

[1] 'I have never such a lively sense of the being, presence, and goodness

Isa. 38:14. 'Lord, I am oppressed! Undertake for me.'

2 Cor. 1:3. 'Blessed be God, even the Father of our Lord Jesus Christ, the Father of mercies, and the God of all comfort, who comforteth us in all our tribulation.'

2 Cor. 1:5. 'As the sufferings of Christ abound in us, so our consolation also aboundeth by Christ.'

> Persecutions borne for Christ by his members are called *'Christ's sufferings'*, for the Head feels what the members endure. So also our sufferings, borne calmly because sent to us by Christ, may be called 'Christ's sufferings in us'. If so, we may enjoy the 'abounding consolation' under ordinary affliction.

2 Cor. 4:17, 18. 'Our light affliction, which is but for a moment, worketh for us a far more exceeding and eternal weight or glory, *while we look not at the things that are seen,* but at the things which are not seen.'

> Sickness and suffering will benefit us, so far as they lead us to take off our eye from things seen, and to fix our eye on our Elder Brother within the veil, and all that is there.

2 Cor. 12:9. 'My grace is sufficient for thee; for my strength is made perfect in weakness.'

> 1. The free love that was 'exceeding abundant' toward Paul on the day it arrested him, renewed him, and made him righteous, is surely sufficient for any emergency. What

---

of God, as in pain, sickness, and suffering.' 'Methinks I hear God say, Take this medicine; it is exactly fitted to the case, prepared and weighed by my own hands.'—*Adams' Private Thoughts.*

is it not capable of doing, if it did this at a time when the man was a rebel! 2. And then, thy want of strength will even be an occasion for his glorious power appearing in the field.

Isa. 49:10. 'He that hath mercy on them shall lead them, even by the springs of water shall he guide them.'[2]

1 John 1:9. 'If we confess our sins, he is faithful and just to forgive us our sins, and to cleanse us from all unrighteousness.'

Psa. 32:5-6. 'I acknowledge my sin unto thee, and mine iniquity have I not hid. I said, I will confess my transgressions unto the Lord, and thou forgavest the iniquity of my sin. For this [*i.e.* since this is so] shall every one that is godly pray unto thee in a time when thou mayest be found: surely in floods of great waters, they shall not come nigh unto him.'

Rom. 8:26-27. 'Likewise the Spirit also helpeth our infirmities [*e.g. our want of ability!*] for we know not what we should pray for as we ought; but the Spirit himself maketh intercession for us with groanings that cannot be uttered. And he that searcheth the hearts knoweth what is the mind of the Spirit, because he maketh intercession for the saints according to the will of God.'

Here is, 1. The Spirit interceding *within us,* on earth; 2.

---

[2] 'I find my Lord going and coming seven times a day. His visits are short, but they are both frequent and sweet.'—*S. Rutherford's Letters.*

Christ interceding *for us,* in heaven; 3. The Father giving heed to what thus comes up before him, in the censer of the Intercessor.

Think of Job 7:13-14. 'When I say, My bed shall comfort me, my couch shall ease my complaint, then thou scarest me with dreams, and terrifiest me through visions.'

1. You see there has nothing overtaken you but what is common to men. 2. All the while, remember 'we have not an High Priest that cannot be touched by a feeling of our infirmities.'

Esther 6:1. 'On that night could not the king sleep; and he commanded to bring the book of records of the Chronicles; and they were read before the king.'

That sleepless night was sent by God for the very end that the king's thoughts might be led, by the records, to Mordecai. What if there be some truth of God, or some view of duty, to which you are to be led by your sleeplessness?

Rom. 15:5. 'The God of patience and consolation.'

Isa. 53:7. 'He was oppressed, and he was afflicted; yet he opened not his mouth.'

1. Christ our atonement. 2. Christ our example.

Psa. 9:13. 'Have mercy upon me, O Lord . . . Thou that liftest me up from the gates of death, that I may shew forth all thy praise in the gates of the daughter of Zion.'

Amos 5:8. 'Seek him that maketh the seven stars and Orion; and turneth the shadow of death into the morning.'

> God of Creation, God of Providence. He can remove the gloomy cloud, and give you instead the bright morn of health.

Isa. 26:3. 'Thou wilt keep him in perfect peace whose mind is stayed on thee, because he trusteth in thee.'

Phil. 2:27. 'For indeed he [Epaphroditus] was sick nigh unto death; but God had mercy on him.'

Isa. 26:4. 'Trust ye in the Lord for ever, for in the Lord Jehovah is the *Rock of Ages*'—(margin).

> The Rock on which you are safe (the true Etam, *Judg.* 15:8) is to be found, not in the world, nor in self, nor in sacraments, nor in prayer, but in Jah Jehovah himself.

> *Rock of Ages, cleft for me!*
> *Let me hide myself in Thee.*
>
> *When I soar to worlds unknown,*
> *See Thee on Thy judgment throne,*
> *Rock of Ages, cleft for me!*
> *Let me hide myself in Thee.*

Song of Sol. 8:6. 'Set me as a seal upon thine heart, as a seal upon thine arm: for love is strong as death; jealousy [*i.e.* jealous love] cruel as the grave' [*i.e.* as tenacious of its rights, and deaf to all remonstrance].

Psa. 119:92. 'Unless thy law [*i.e.* thy revealed truth] had been my delight, I should have perished in mine affliction.'[3]

Luke 18:13. 'God be merciful to me a sinner!'

> Baxter on his deathbed, many times prayed this prayer. He said, 'God may justly condemn me for the best duty I ever did; all my hopes are from the free mercy of God in Christ.'

Heb. 12:10. 'But he [chastens] for our profit, that we may be *partakers of his holiness.*'

Joel 1:19. 'O Lord, to thee will I cry; for fire hath devoured pastures of the wilderness.'

2 Chron. 16:12. 'And Asa, in the thirty and ninth year of his reign, was diseased in his feet, until his disease was exceeding great; yet in his disease he sought not to the Lord, but to the physicians.'

> Saints, not only in paroxysms of pain, but in long-continued sickness, may practically be saying, 'Why should I wait on the Lord any further?' Lord, keep me from falling!

2 Tim. 4:20. 'Trophimus have I left at Miletum sick.'

1 Tim. 5:23. 'Thine often infirmities.'

> 1. Christ, who delayed for a time to visit Lazarus, often declines to heal the sicknesses of his most useful and

---

[3] Sitting in my blankets, with this Bible before me, I seem like old Elwes, with a bushel of bank notes and India bonds; but with this difference, that he must have his all taken away, and I shall have mine with me.' — *Cecil, Fragment written in Illness.*

beloved labourers. 2. And, as in the case of Lazarus, it is 'for the glory of God'. Hence he gave no power to Paul to heal Trophimus, or Timothy; nor to John to heal Gaius (*3 John*).

2 Kings 20:7. 'Take a lump of figs. And they took it, and laid it on the boil, and he recovered.'

Means are used, and means are blessed of God, as it seems good to him. 'My times are in thy hands.'—Psa. 31:15.

Introduction to Chapter 2

The Sick Believer Troubled

HERE the visitor cannot but feel his need of the present power of the Holy Spirit; for without him he will be to the tempted, and to the troubled of any kind, as Job's friends were to him, 'miserable comforter'. Call to mind, therefore, that God gives joy and peace 'by the power of the Holy Ghost'.—(*Rom.* 15:13.) Lord, come.

Let me, thus prefacing my work of faith, go forward:—1. I may be speaking to the tempted. I may seasonably remind him of the experience of others in such cases; *e.g.* I may tell him of that saying of Jeremy Taylor, 'Not to be tempted is sometimes the most subtle temptation.' Or I may take up a text such as Luke 22:31, 'Satan has desired to sift you.' I may briefly point out such thoughts as these:—*a.* See, here is Christ standing by his tempted ones! The rack would be no rack, if he bathed me all the while in his love. *b.* See, here is Christ praying for you! *c.* See, Satan is doing work *for you;* he is sifting away what in you is chaff. *d.* See, the whole process is under Christ's eye.

2. I may be speaking to one troubled about his special malady. It seems to him anger; like a frown of God upon him. Well, I take up (let us say) Psa. 6:3, 'Thou, O Lord, how long?' (1.) I pray with him, helping him to cry thus. And perhaps I pray specially, that if there be any real ground for his suspicions as to God's frown, the sin may be made plain; for medicine is applied in vain so long as the arrow head is in the wound. (2.) At the same time, I do not leave him thus, but I bid him at all events fix his thoughts upon 'THOU LORD'. Think of the love of him who gave Christ; and then cry, 'How long?' Love must have great reasons for continuing to try you.

3. The believer is under strong pain. I will help him: *a*. By words and looks of sympathy. *b*. I will use, such hints as Lam. 3:33, 'He doth not *willingly* afflict.' God reigns; there is some profound reason, which divine wisdom could reveal, for this pain and every moment of its continuance. *c*. Perhaps I may see it right to suggest that it is not sent by way of penalty, for this is not the scene of retribution, and a believer suffers only in order to sanctification. *d*. I will pray with him, and that tenderly, though briefly. *e*. I will go from him to pray for him.

Old Zacbary Boyd's *Last Battle of the Soul in Death,* gives many happy hints as to such cases.

2

The Sick Believer Troubled

I. By Temptation

1 Cor. 10:13. 'There hath no temptation taken you but such as is common to man; but God is faithful, who will not suffer you to be tempted above that ye are able.'[1] Connect with this passage the text in—

Luke 22:31. 'Behold, Satan hath desired to sift you as wheat . . . But I have prayed for thee.'

Psa. 103:13-14. 'The Lord pitieth them that fear him; for he knoweth our frame.'

Exod. 3:7. 'I know their sorrows; and I am come down to deliver them.'

Rev. 12:11. 'They overcame him by the blood of the Lamb, and by the word of their testimony.'

---

[1] 'No man is less beloved because he is tempted.'—*Brooks*. Think of Job; yea, think of the Lord Jesus.

If Satan say that I am deserving wrath; I reply, 'Most true, I am *worthy* even of everlasting death; but I am *warranted,* nevertheless, to expect everlasting life, because *the blood of the Lamb* answers every charge against me.'

Rom. 16:20. 'The God of peace shall bruise Satan under your feet shortly.'

The God who put an end to the warfare between himself and you by the cross, shall soon put an end to the warfare between you and Satan by giving you the crown.

Luke 13:16. 'Ought not this woman, being a daughter of Abraham, whom Satan hath bound, lo, these eighteen years, be loosed from this bond on the Sabbath day?'

1. Christ speaks in the tone of authority, as the Woman's Seed who bruises the serpent's head. 2. He intimates his determination to take what prey he pleases from Satan. 3. He does it on the Sabbath; giving rest on the day of rest in his character of Giver of rest.

Psa. 91:13-14. 'Thou shalt tread upon the lion and the adder; the young lion and the dragon shalt thou trample under feet. Because he hath set his love upon me, therefore will I deliver him: I will set him on high because he hath known my name.'

1. There are to be lions in the path, but there is to be victory over them. 2. Deliverance is promised to you, not because of your strength, or services, or merit, or fervent prayers, but because you delight in him who loved you. 3. Exaltation, also, will follow your going down into the valley of

humiliation, simply because you perceive and apprehend the grace of your redeeming God, 'knowing his name'. 4. Christ trod this same path; for the Psalm was specially spoken by the Head for the sake of the members.

James 1:12. 'Blessed is the man that endureth temptation; for when he is tried, he shall receive the crown of life which the Lord promised to them that love him.'

Zech. 3:1-2. 'And he shewed me Joshua the High Priest standing before the angel of the Lord, and Satan standing at his right hand to resist him. And the Lord said unto Satan, The Lord rebuke thee, O Satan; even the Lord that hath chosen Jerusalem rebuke thee: is not this a brand plucked out of the fire?'

> 1. Satan's daring malignity. 2. The tender care of the Angel of the Covenant. 3. The Lord's right to save whom he will. 4. The Lord's glorying in his saved ones.

Mark 1:11-12. 'And there came a voice from heaven, saying, Thou art my beloved Son, in whom I am well pleased. And immediately the Spirit driveth him into the wilderness; and he was there forty days tempted of Satan.'

> A long season of the sorest and most cunning temptations of hell followed a short season of unspeakable delight.

Luke 11:22. 'A stronger than he shall come upon him and overcome him.'

1 Pet. 5:9. 'Whom resist.' But how? 'Stedfast in the faith',—looking away from the Tempter to Jesus.

Heb. 11:14-15. 'Forasmuch then as the children are partakers of flesh and blood, he also himself likewise took part of the same; that through death he might destroy him that had the power of death, that is, the devil; and deliver them who through fear of death were all their lifetime subject to bondage.'

> 1. An incarnate Saviour, entering into his children's state of weakness and temptation. 2. His death giving Satan's power a death-wound. 3. His victory intended to free from bondage souls that were in dismal bondage up to the time when he visited them. 4. Through his death and victory our life may now be full of peace. 5. When fear returns, let us return to this conqueror.[2]

Heb. 2:18. 'In that he suffered, being tempted, he is able to succour them that are tempted.'

Job 13:15. 'Though he slay me, yet will I trust in him.'

2 Cor. 12:7, 9. The messenger of Satan to buffet me, lest I should be exalted above measure . . . Most gladly, therefore, will I rather glory in mine infirmities.'

---

[2] 'Be not surprised that, in the approach of death, Satan should roar against you and assault you in new forms . . . But cast yourself resolutely into the arms of a frowning God, believing the holy love of his heart, and his resting in the sweet savour and overcoming excellency of the sacrifice of Jesus, whom he beholds on high pleading for your support, victory, and glorification.'—*Love's Letters*, p. 135

Psa. 31:15. 'My times are in thy hand.'

Psa. 25:15. Mine eyes are ever toward the Lord, for he shall pluck my feet out of the net.'

II. BY CIRCUMSTANCES CONNECTED WITH HIS SICKNESS

Psa. 65:5. 'By terrible things in righteousness wilt thou answer us, O God of our salvation; who art the confidence of all the ends of the earth, and of them that are afar off upon the sea.'

> 1. God often visits the soul with providences which, either by their strangeness or their greatness, fill it with awe. 2. He may be answering former prayers in so doing. 3. He is certainly acting righteously. 4. It is he, not the creature, that is the object of our confidence. 5. He is so, when our eye discerns him as God of salvation—God able to save by power and grace, because of his beloved Son. All this, though we were at earth's end, and tossed on the wildest sea.

Psa. 6:3. 'My soul is also sore vexed! But thou, O Lord, how long?'

Judg. 6:13-14. 'O my Lord, if the Lord be with us, why then is all this befallen us? and where all his miracles which our fathers told us of, saying, Did not the Lord bring us up from Egypt? But now the Lord hath forsaken us, and delivered us into the hands of the Midianites. And the Lord looked on him, and said, Go in this thy might.'

> 1. Most of our difficulties arise from discussing what belongs to God, not to us. 2. God does not reason with us, but replies to our suspicious reasoning by displaying anew the love of his heart and the power of his arm.

Phil. 2:1. 'If there be therefore any consolation in Christ, if any comfort of love, if any fellowship of the Spirit, if any bowels [affection] and mercies'—

> As if he had said, 'If there be any light in the sun, use it.' Whatever be your outward state, and whatever it suggests to your suspicious soul, remember—1. In Christ there is *consolation* to all that mourn, reaching to the depth of the soul, for it shows your conscience that God is satisfied with that doing and dying of Christ which he bids you know and believe. 2. In Christ you reach the sweet solace of the Father's love also. 3. In Christ you find the Spirit has brought you into fellowship with the Father and the Son, and makes you of one mind with God. 4. In Christ you find that you, the chief of sinners, and, it may be, the most tossed and vexed of men, have 'bowels [affection] and mercies' for your pillow. Ay, 'bowels and mercies' have ordered every trying circumstance of your case.

Rom. 7:24-25. 'O wretched man that I am, who shall deliver me from the body of this death? [*q.d.*, 'O my sin, my sin! This is worse than death! O this loathsome carcase of sin! O this death that is ever weakening the life eternal! But there is help for me in the Saviour.'] I thank God through Jesus Christ our Lord!'

The storm is chang'd into a calm
  at his command and will;
So that the waves, which rag'd before,
  now quiet are and still.

(Psalm 107:29, *Scottish Psalter* 1650.)

Isa. 38:1. 'In those days was Hezekiah sick unto death
. . . And Hezekiah wept sore.'

> Whether it was that he desired to live longer for the sake
> of God's cause (verse 18-19), or whether it was that he
> thought he saw a frown on the face of his God in that
> disease, or whether it was the natural shrinking of the
> flesh from death, we know not, but there was a 'thorn in
> his flesh'. This led him to the Lord.

Isa. 38:3. 'Remember now, O Lord, I beseech thee, how
I have walked before thee in truth, and with a perfect heart,
have done that which is good in thy sight!'

> Lord, I am thine wholly; as I have sought to show by my
> life, not merely on a deathbed! I have impartially sought to
> comply with thy revealed will, using the atoning sacrifices
> and honouring thy commandments. 'Remember me with
> the favour thou bearest to thine own!' (*Psa.* 106:4.)

Isa. 38:20. 'The Lord was ready to save me. Therefore
we will sing my songs to the stringed instruments, all the
days of our life, in the house of the Lord.'

Gen. 49:23, 24. 'The archers have sorely grieved him
and shot at him, and hated him. But his bow abode in
strength, and the arms of his hands were made strong by
the hands of the mighty God of Jacob.'

Mal. 3:2. 'He is like a refiner's fire, and like fuller's soap.'

2 Tim. 4:22. 'The Lord Jesus Christ be with thy spirit.'

> Christ personally as well as officially; Christ with all he is and has.

Mark 4:40. 'Why are ye so fearful! How is it that ye have no faith?'[3]

Psa. 27:13. 'Unless I had believed to see the goodness of the Lord in the land of the living.'

> Who can tell what would have happened, had I not been led to rest my soul on Jehovah's covenant love?

Psa. 31:22. 'For I said in my haste [*i.e.* while fleeing in haste from foes, as Israel from Pharaoh on the Passover night], I am cut off from before thine eyes; nevertheless thou heardest the voice of my supplications when I cried unto thee. [As Israel was heard at the Red Sea.] O love the Lord, all ye his saints.'

Psa. 77:2-4, 6-11. 'In the day of my trouble I sought the Lord. I remembered God and was troubled. I am so troubled that I cannot speak . . . I commune with mine own heart. Will the Lord cast off for ever? and will he be favourable no more? is his mercy clean gone for ever?

---

[3] 'Sin is too bitter when it makes thee forget that Christ is sweet.' — Durant. 'True humility consists more in believing, than in being sensible of sin.' — *Owen*.

doth his promise fail for evermore? Hath God forgotten to be gracious? hath he in anger shut up his tender mercies? *Selah*. And I said this is my infirmity . . . The years of the right hand of the Most High! I will remember the works of the Lord: surely I will remember thy wonders of old.'

> 1. To forget self and surrounding circumstances, and then to fix the eye intently on the Lord, whose works in days past have been so fragrant with mercy, this is true relief for a downcast soul. 2. Especially now, when we can remember those 'years of his right hand', in which his beloved Son walked on earth, dividing our Red Sea, rending the veil by being rent himself. O Calvary, Calvary! O years of the right hand of the Most High!

Lam. 3:19-22. 'Remembering mine affliction and my misery, the wormwood and the gall.[4] My soul hath them still in remembrance, and is humbled in me. This I recall to my mind, therefore have I hope. It is of the Lord's mercies that we are not consumed, because his compassions fail not.'

Psa. 119:113. 'I hate vain thoughts; but thy law do I love.'

> 1. Notice, it is, 'I hate *thoughts*', in opposition to God's undoubted discovery of his mind and heart. I hate my own fancies, my own heart's imaginations; I hate suspicions and surmises. 2. Instead of these, I rest my soul on his 'law'—his

---

[4] 'When saints are under trials and well humbled, little sins raise great cries in the conscience; and in prosperity, conscience is a hope that gives dispensations to our heart.'—*S. Rutherford*.

revelation—his manifestation of himself, by word and by deed, as the Saviour of the guilty who set to their seal that he is well-pleased in his Son.[5]

Rom. 15:13. 'Now the God of hope fill you with all joy and peace in believing, that ye may abound in hope, through the power of the Holy Ghost.'

Not *after* having believed, but *while* you are in the act of looking to the root of Jesse, verse 12.

III. Under Bodily Pain

Job 5:6-10. 'Affliction cometh not forth of the dust, neither doth trouble spring out of the ground . . . I would seek unto God, and unto God would I commit my cause; which doeth great things and unsearchable . . . who giveth rain upon the earth.'

Lam. 3:32. 'Though he cause grief, yet will he have compassion according to the multitude of his mercies.'

Lam. 3:33. 'For he doth not willingly afflict nor grieve the children of men.'

It is in order to attain some great end that he sends that agonising pain; otherwise he would no more have sent it

---

[5] 'It was good for me to come hither to learn a new mystery of Christ, that *Christ's promise is to be believed against all appearances.*'— *S. Rutherford.*

than a tender mother would put her babe on the rack. 'Love will not wrong us. There shall be no needless suffering.'

Mark 15:23. 'And they gave him to drink wine mingled with myrrh; and he received it not.'

1. This myrrh cup would have deadened his bodily pain; but *he* behoved to suffer the uttermost, in body and soul. 2. But as for us, we may use every alleviation; since believing in him, our curse is done away. 3. He purchased alleviation for us.

Luke 23:40, 42. 'But the other, answering, rebuked him . . . And he said unto Jesus, Lord, remember me when thou comest into thy kingdom.'

His excruciating bodily agony is forgotten in the intense earnestness of his soul's longing after God.[6]

Col. 1:11-12. 'Strengthened with all might, according to his glorious power, unto all patience and long-suffering with joyfulness; giving thanks unto the Father which hath made us meet to be partakers of the inheritance of the saints in light.'

Here is, 1. Patience imparted, such patience as the Lord's glorious power wrought in the martyrs, in the dying thief, and in thousands of others; 2. Patience as the result of the Lord's secret might strengthening you; 3. Joyfulness as the topstone to patience! 4. Thanksgiving for being made meet for glory — one of the tributary streams that swell this river of patience and long-suffering.

---

[6] Baxter on his deathbed: 'I have pain, there is no arguing against sense; but I have peace, I have peace.'

John 19:32. 'Then came the soldiers and brake the legs of the first; and of the other which was crucified with him.'

> See! The converted thief, that saved man, on his way to paradise, and very near it now; see, nevertheless, how the Lord allows his body to be mangled. O what racking, distracting pain to him! And yet, see how the Lord loved him, ready within an hour to bathe him in bliss. Perhaps, something of this is included in the expression, 'Thy life given thee as a prey' (*Jer.* 21:9; 38:2; 39:18; 45:5).

Acts 16:23-25. 'Many stripes upon them . . . Their feet fast in the stocks . . . And at midnight, Paul and Silas prayed and sang praises unto God.'

Heb. 11:32-37. 'The time would fail me to tell of Gideon, &c., who through faith [*i.e.* by fixing their eye on God their deliverer, 12:2] subdued kingdoms . . . were tortured, not accepting deliverance, that they might obtain a better resurrection. They were stoned, they were sawn asunder.'

Dan. 3:25. 'Lo, I see four men loose, walking in the midst of the fire, and they have no hurt; and the form of the fourth is like the Son of God.'[7]

Mal. 3:3. 'He shall sit as a refiner and purifier of silver.'[8]

Ezra 9:13. 'Though our God has punished us less than our iniquities deserve.'

---

[7] 'His sweet presence eateth out the bitterness of sorrow.'—*S. Rutherford.*
[8] 'Sin the disease, Christ the physician, pain the medicine.'—*Cecil.*

Matt. 11:5-6. 'The blind receive their sight, and the lame walk; the lepers are cleansed, and the deaf hear; the dead are raised up, and the poor have the gospel preached to them. And blessed is he whosoever shall not be offended in me.'

> 1. Christ has at this moment the same eye-salve that gave sight to the blind, the same strength that he imparted to the lame, the same health that made lepers whole, the same life that made the dead arise; so that he could relieve you, if he would. 2. He sees it better, however, to leave you lingering and suffering, as he did the Baptist. 3. But, meanwhile, to you the good news is sent, *viz.*, pardon through his blood to your guilty soul, and the merit of his obedience imputed to you, that you may be clothed in righteousness, and his Spirit imparted. 4. Be not stumbled at his dealings in providence. At his coming again, if not now, these mists of providence shall all be cleared. Payson was asked if he saw any particular reason for his sore distress, 'No; but I am as well satisfied as if I could see a thousand; God's will is the very perfection of all reason.'

Rom. 7:35. 'Who shall separate us from the love of Christ [*i.e.* from his love toward us]? Shall tribulation or distress?' [These separate our thoughts too much from him; but not him from thinking on us.]

Deut. 32:36. 'For the Lord shall judge his people, and repent himself for his servants, when he seeth that their power is gone.'

> Deliverance is nearest when affliction is at its height.

John 9:3. 'Jesus answered, Neither hath this man sinned, nor his parents; but that the works of God should be made manifest in him.'

> His special affliction is not caused by special sin in him, but is the result of a special design of God to glory himself in this man's case.

Luke 21:19. 'In your patience possess ye your souls.'

> By being patient, win or save your souls; *i.e.* make no shipwreck of your souls by impatience, whatever you meet with.[9]

Heb. 112:2. 'Looking unto Jesus, the author and finisher of faith, who for the joy that was set before him endured the cross, despising the shame, and is set down on the right hand of the throne of God.'

> Here is, 1. Christ's atoning work; 2. Christ strengthened in the midst of his sharpest pains by the thought of the kingdom; 3. Christ now at rest in glory; 4. Christ an example to us in the manner of bearing suffering; 5. Christ able to yield us sympathy under pain; 6. Christ pointing the sufferer to the crown of glory and the throne.

1 Pet. 5:10-11. 'But the God of all grace, who hath called us into his eternal glory by Christ Jesus, after that

---

[9] A man of God could say, 'Blessed be God for all his favours, and particularly for the special mercy of the stone!' The will of my God may put me to pain; but it is the will of God.'—*Adams' Private Thoughts.* He says also, 'By pain God drives me to prayer, teaches me what prayer is, inclines me to pray . . . Say, my heart, with respect to the stone, I am unworthy of this mercy!'

ye have suffered a while, make you perfect, stablish, strengthen, settle you: to him be glory and dominion for ever and ever. Amen.'

> Let us see how the 'God of all grace' has enabled his own 'to suffer a while'. Payson wrote 'Death comes every night and stands by my bed in the form of terrible convulsions, every one of which threatens to separate the soul from the body. These continue to grow more and more till every bone is dislocated with pain, leaving me with the certainty that I shall have it all to endure again the next night . . . I have suffered twenty times as much as I could in being burnt at the stake, while my joy in God so abounded as to render my sufferings not only tolerable but welcome . . . While my body is thus tortured, the soul is perfectly, perfectly happy and peaceful—more happy than I can possibly express to you.'
>
> Think of all this, and also of the result, 'made perfect, stablished, strengthened, settled!'

INTRODUCTION TO CHAPTER 3

THE BELIEVER IS DYING

IN his dying hour Stephen was 'full of the Holy Ghost' (*Acts* 7:55), and hence his triumphant departure with Christ full in view. Remember that we who go to visit a dying believer need to be thus led by the Spirit ourselves, if we are to help the dying one.

1. Let us aim at keeping the dying one at '*the beginning of his confidence*' (*Heb*. 3:14). Dying Baxter thanked God for the publican's prayer, 'O God, be merciful to me, a sinner.' Let us seek to fix the eye on the *sacrifice for sin*, and on *him who offered it*—not on the person's good deeds, useful life, long experience, proved graces. Let us point him to Paul in 2 Tim. 1:12: 'I know whom I have believed, and am persuaded that he is able to keep that which I have committed to him against that day.'

2. Let us help the dying one to realise Christ as the friend on yonder shore, waiting for his arrival. A personal Saviour, the Elder Brother, the Lord Jesus full of grace and truth, full of sympathy—these are views of him such as one needs in going *alone* into that other world.

3. Let us avoid generalities. It is not desirable even to speak much of the rest and the glories of another world. At least, at such a time the soul is better fed with the Lord Jesus, the Righteous One, in whom we are accepted. Let us learn from that dying believer who said, 'I like to *hear* of the beauties of heaven, but I do not *dwell* on them. *Christ will be there; this is what I dwell upon.*'

4. Let us *speak little,* and suggest texts rather than make remarks of our own. One who touched the waters of Jordan says: 'It appeared to me that at a dying hour, the proper exercise of the soul is that of *calm waiting* and sure expectation of the coming salvation, rather than the performance of a multiplicity of devotional exercises.' 'Why criest thou unto me? Fear not; stand still and see the salvation of God.'

5. Let us pray *briefly,* in Scripture style, tenderly and fervently. If 'full of the Holy Ghost' and able to realise Jesus waiting to receive his departing Lazarus, with what holy calmness would we then pray!

6. We may take occasion, at the same time to remind the believer that this is his *last* opportunity of glorifying his God on earth, and that it is a *special* opportunity; as his words will be so well remembered. Let him, as he is able, commend his God and Saviour to his household, and friends that come to see him. Let him manifest to all the power of a believed gospel and a Saviour trusted in. Let him pray for the church of God.

3

THE BELIEVER IS DYING

Rom. 14:7-8. 'For none of us [believers] liveth to himself, and no man dieth to himself. For whether we live, we live unto the Lord; and whether we die, we die unto the Lord: whether we live, therefore, or die, we are the Lord's.'[1]

Rev. 1:18. 'I am he that liveth, and was dead; and, behold, I am alive for evermore, Amen; and have the keys of hell [*the unseen world*] and of death.'

John 14:19. 'The world seeth me no more, but ye see me; because I live, ye shall live also.'

Rom. 5:10. 'Much more, being reconciled, we shall be saved by his life.'

> Christ is now living above to apply his finished work, and attend to every wound, want, wish, of his redeemed ones. It is he, also, that shall meet us when we land on yonder foreign shore.

[1] It is not right to pray for death. The will of God is better than death.'—*Mrs Hawkes.*

Luke 2:29. 'Lord now lettest thou [thou art letting] thy servant depart in peace, according to thy word, for mine eyes have seen thy salvation.'

> How appropriately are these words sung on leaving the Lord's table by the communicants in the French Protestant Church! Looking on Christ who lived and died, the just for the unjust, we may surely depart from this life, as well as from any of its shifting scenes in peace. A Waldensian martyr sang these words at the stake remembering how he had sung them at the Lord's table in other days.

Psa. 119:151. 'Thou art near, O Lord.'

Psa. 23:4. 'Thou art with me.'

Heb. 10:19, 21. 'Having boldness to enter into the holiest, by the blood of Jesus . . . And having an high priest over the house of God.'

> Two things give a sinner boldness in going to the Holy One in the full blaze of his holiness: 1. *The blood of Jesus;* he poured out his life, and so the Father, looking on that outpoured life, can justly say to us who point to the same, 'Live!' 2. *Jesus himself,* the living Priest; he leads us in by his Spirit, and presents himself for us, the One for all who come. 3. And these same grounds of boldness are enough for us when we leave the body and pass into the immediate presence of the Holy One.[2]

Psa. 17:15. 'As for me, I will behold thy face in right-

---

[2] A minister in London, in 1832, thus expressed himself on his deathbed: 'Christ in his person, Christ in his offices, Christ in the love of his heart, Christ in the power of his arm—and now [gently reclining his head upon the pillow], Death, strike!'

eousness: I shall be satisfied, when I awake, with thy likeness.'

Psa. 16:8-10. 'He is at my right hand; I shall not be moved. Therefore my heart is glad, and my glory rejoiceth; my flesh also shall rest in hope; for thou wilt not leave my soul in hell; neither wilt thou suffer thine Holy One to see corruption.'

> Realise your union to Christ. Christ sang this, and to him it applies primarily. But it is true also of every member of his in a modified sense. 1. Commit your flesh to the grave in full hope of the resurrection of the just. 2. Be sure that he will bring back your soul to the body, and not leave you in corruption. 3. Let the prospect of this resurrection gladden you amid disease and the accompaniments of death that nature shrinks from.

1 Cor. 3:21-22. 'All things are yours; whether Paul, or Apollos, or Cephas, or the world, or life, or death, or things present, or things to come; all are yours; and ye are Christ's; and Christ is God's.'

Eph. 3:16. 'That he would grant you, according to the riches of his glory, to be strengthened with all might, by his Spirit in the inner man.'

John 17:11. 'And now I am no more in the world, but these are in the world, and I come to thee. Holy Father, keep through thine own name those whom thou hast given me.'

> Our Lord's words. But a member may appropriate the

words of the Head. You may thus, in all reverence, speak to your Father, thinking of those you leave behind.

2 Sam. 18:5. 'Though my house be not so with God; yet he hath made me an everlasting covenant, ordered in all things and sure.'

> Think of the *covenant,* the free-grace-arrangement God has made with your soul. Sovereign love chose you! called you! justified you! is sanctifying you! and will soon glorify you. He that has made such an arrangement with your soul may well be left to arrange your household. 'I saw not', says Bishop Cooper, 'I saw not my children when they were in the womb, yet there the Lord fed them without my care and knowledge. I shall not see them when I go out of the body, yet they shall not want or suffer.'

Psa. 31:5. 'Into thy hands I commit my spirit.' Luke 23:46.

> The Master's words on the cross! And ours, too! both in life and death. So close is the sympathy and fellowship.

Heb. 13:8. 'Jesus Christ the same yesterday, and to-day, and for ever.'

Deut. 34:5. 'So Moses, the Servant of the Lord, died there, in the land of Moab, according to the word of the Lord; and he buried him.'

> Moses had just sung, Deut. 33:26, 'There is none like the God of Jeshurun . . . The eternal God is thy refuge,[3] and

---

[3] One says: 'When I was told I had probably but a few hours to live I felt on the edge of eternity without any assured hope of an interest in Christ. I could not remember a time when I had even a desire to come to him;

underneath are the everlasting arms.' And so he is laid to rest. And lo! fifteen hundred years afterwards, how safe he is! how blessed! for, 'There appeared unto them Elias with Moses: and they were talking with Jesus' (*Mark* 9:4).

Josh. 23:14. 'And, behold, this day I am going the way of all the earth; and ye know in all your hearts, and in all your souls, that not one thing hath failed of all the good things which the Lord your God spake concerning you; all are come to pass unto you, and not one thing hath failed thereof.'

1 Cor. 15:26, 55. 'The last enemy-death . . . O death where is thy sting? O grave, where is thy victory? The sting of death is sin: and the strength of sin is the law. But thanks be to God, who giveth us the victory through our Lord Jesus Christ.'

> In such a moment as death, our eye must rest on nothing but Jesus. Not on self, not on past experience not on our having once believed, but altogether and directly on him whom we are about to see, face to face. Neither are we to look on death, nor think of its sting; we are to think of him who has made death 'a stingless serpent, a powerless enemy: a lion whose great teeth are broken'. Think your last thought in the body on God clothed in our nature, dying for our sins, and living to receive us home. 'I well remember', says one, 'the feelings of perturbation which

---

and I was thus obliged to cast myself with all my sins and nothingness upon him; and then I found peace! Christ's is a finished work, or I do not know what would become of me.'—*Simple Record of the Grace of God*, 1833.

seized me when I had the first attack which brought me into such close contact with the world of spirits. It appeared to me strange that *death*, of which I had heard only by report, should at last have seized me. It was so sudden that I had no time to collect or compose my mind by those views which are contained in the gospel, and my first impression was great alarm—a total breaking down of the whole mind, so that I seemed to myself the victim of vengeance. My first feeling was therefore flight, rather than to seize the defensive armour of the gospel, to escape from the terrible assault of that sore enemy . . . When the cloud passed away, I recollect well how vast the work of Christ appeared in my eyes! It seemed to me to be an impossible thing that I could perish; *and the gospel salvation appeared to me like a great continent,* stretching out as far as my eyes could see, ready to receive me.'—*Thoughts in Prospect of Death*, pp. 5-6.

Phil. 1:20. 'Christ shall be magnified in my body, whether it be by life, or by death.'

Phil. 1:21. 'To die is gain.'

Phil. 1:23. 'To depart and be with Christ, which is far better.'

John 21:19. 'This spake he, signifying by what death he should glorify God. And when he had spoken this, he saith unto him, Follow me.'

Heb. 11:22. 'By faith Joseph, when he died, made mention of the departing of the children of Israel; and gave commandment concerning his bones.'

Looking by faith within the veil, and seeing things to come, he anticipated joyfully the fulfilment of every promise made to the fathers.

Heb. 11:21. 'By faith Jacob, when he was adying, . . . worshipped, leaning on the top of his staff.'

> 1. With *his staff* he passed over Jordan, a poor stranger—leaning on his staff, therefore, he recalls God's mercies during his long pilgrimage. 2. He adores, in lively faith, him for whose salvation he was waiting.

Rev. 14:13. 'Blessed are the dead which die in the Lord from henceforth; Yea, saith the Spirit, that they may rest from their labours; and their works do follow them.'

> 1. The soul 'in the Lord', under the shadow of the Great Rock, to which it first fled weary and woeful, now falls asleep under that shadow. 2. The Father's voice from the light inaccessible cries, 'Blessed'. 3. The Holy Spirit, who is to raise up the body (*Rom.* 8:11), and fully sanctify the soul, responds, 'Yea', and speaks of the labour he enabled that believer to engage in for God, and of the reward with which that labour shall be crowned.

2 Tim 1:12. 'I know whom I have believed, and am persuaded that he is able to keep that which I have committed unto him against that day.'[4]

[4] Cecil speaks thus: 'When one of my physicians told me, with many tears, that I must die—my soul, like a man suddenly overwhelmed with an inundation, looked about hastily to examine the ground on which it stood to meet the expected trial. But the ground was in a moment found to be such as could secure me from any flood, and I was enabled to say, "My friend, you do not at all alarm me, for I know whom I have believed, and I am persuaded that he is able to keep that which I have

No trust to any labours, attainments, revelations, services, holiness, duties; his eye does not rest on his apostleship, nor on his apostolic knowledge and gifts. Christ alone is in his thoughts. Nor is it either the strength or weakness of his faith that he is pondering; he is pondering the object of faith, and his ability to save and keep his saved ones, his matchless qualifications to meet the case and circumstances of a sinner living or dying.

Psa. 116:15. 'Precious in the sight of the Lord is the death of his saints.'

Everything, therefore, connected with it is interesting to him—the disease, its every turn, your pain, your languor, your weariness, your cares, &c.

Psa. 48:14. 'This God is our God for ever and ever; he will be our guide even unto death.'

'*Unto* death', and *over* death;

> *Not one object of his care*
> *Ever suffered shipwreck there.*

Job 14:13-14. 'Oh that thou wouldest hide me in the grave . . . All the days of my appointed time will I wait till my change come.'

---

committed to him unto that day." But in going home in the coach by myself, and *looking from off the Rock* on which I stood *to the waves* which surrounded it, my coolness forsook me; I thought of my wife and children, and burst into tears; I thought, too, of my church. The whole was too much, and I was obliged to turn my eyes again *from the waves to the Rock,* and transact with God for my own soul.'—*Fragment written in Illness.*

Oh lay me up among thy treasures when I leave the body. I will wait [*q.d.* on thy mountain of myrrh and hill of frankincense, *Song of Sol.* 4:6; amidst the fragrance of him who is at thy right hand] till the Resurrection come, when 'we shall all be changed.'

Job 19:25-27. 'For I know that my Redeemer liveth, and that he shall stand at the latter day upon the earth; and though after my skin worms destroy this body, yet in my flesh shall I see God: whom I shall see for myself, and mine eyes shall behold, and not another.'

2 Thess. 2:1. 'Our gathering together in him'.

2 Cor. 5:6. 'While at home in the body, we are absent from the Lord.'

Rev. 21:4. 'They shall see his face, and his name shall be on their foreheads.'

Isa. 26:19. 'Thy dead men shall live. My dead body, they shall arise. Awake and sing, ye that dwell in dust.'

The Lord calls the believing dead, *'His dead body'!*

Rom. 8:19, 23. 'For the earnest expectation of the creature waiteth for the manifestation of the sons of God . . . And not only they, but ourselves also, which have the first-fruits of the Spirit, even we ourselves groan within ourselves, waiting for the adoption, to wit, the redemption of our body.'

2 Cor. 5:4. 'For we that are in this tabernacle do groan; being burdened: not for that we would be unclothed, but clothed upon, that mortality might be swallowed up of life.'

> It is no duty in us to desire death, which is a part of the curse. No wonder, then, if we shrink from being 'unclothed'. Our desire should be to get the resurrection body, and the life that shall flow into us then.

1 Cor. 15:42-44. 'It is sown in corruption, it is raised in incorruption: it is sown in dishonour, it is raised in glory: it is sown in weakness, it is raised in power: it is sown a natural body, it is raised a spiritual body.'

> The dead body is a seed, from which is to spring up something very wonderful.

1 Cor. 15:49. 'We shall also bear the image of the heavenly.'

Phil. 3:21. 'Who shall change our vile body, that it may be fashioned like unto his glorious body, according to the working whereby he is able even to subdue all things unto himself.'

1 John 3:2. 'Beloved, now are we the sons of God; and it doth not yet appear what we shall be; but we know that, when he shall appear, we shall be like him; for we shall see him as he is.'

> 'Ye will not sleep long in the dust before the Day break. It is a far shorter piece of the night to you than to Abraham and Moses.'—*S. Rutherford.*

2 Tim. 4:8. 'There is laid up for me a crown of righteousness, which the Lord, the righteous judge, shall give to me at that day; and not to me only, but unto all those also that love his appearing.'

> The reward shall be given as a thing most righteous, purchased by the Righteous One, and given to his justified, to whose service on earth he promised a crown. Yet they will also feel as T. Hooker, who, when one said, 'You are going to receive the reward of your labours', replied, 'Brother, I am going to receive *mercy*.'

John 6:39. 'This is the Father's will which hath sent me, that of all which he hath given me I should lose nothing [not one of them, and nothing of theirs, not a hair of their head even], but should raise it up at the last day.'

Acts 7:56, 59-60. 'Behold, I see the heavens opened, and the Son of man standing on the right hand of God . . . Lord Jesus, receive my spirit . . . Lord, lay not this sin to their charge. And when he had said this, he fell asleep.'

Introduction to Chapter 4

The Sick Person's Spiritual State Is Unknown to You

IF in any case, surely now in this, we need the guidance of the Spirit 'who *searches all things*'. — (*1 Cor.* 2:10.) Let us approach the sick bed of the man, praying such a prayer as Acts 1:24, 'Thou, Lord, which knowest the hearts of all men, shew—'; or 1 Kings 8:39, 'Give to every man according to his ways, whose heart thou knowest; for thou, even thou only, knowest the hearts of all the children of men.'

1. Such persons may be making an erroneous use of James 5:16, 'The effectual fervent *prayer of a righteous man availeth much.*' Let us, therefore, take care to caution them on this point. Let us show that these words are originally, *a.* Spoken to *believers* concerning *believers*; *b.* Spoken about the *recovery* of such from their *disease*; *c.* Spoken in regard to prayer in which *the sick man joins*:

for this is implied by verse 13, where the sick is himself to pray, also; 'Let him pray.' This passage goes no further, and so gives no countenance to any superstitious idea of the effect of good men's prayers. We must not forget to add that the Lord does hear the prayer of his own in behalf of unconverted ones only occasionally, not always; and that the sign of such prayers being heard is this, the person prayed for begins to feel sin, and to look on Christ and pray like the publican and the dying thief.

2. We may deal with those to whom this chapter refers in the way of *asking questions*. This is 'feeling their pulse'. It may be we shall not succeed well in this attempt; but let us try. Our questions may at least cause thought.

3. We may ofttimes get hints from friends about their state.

4. In any case we cannot err in taking up such a passage as John 3:3, and 3:35-36, 'Except a man be born again . . . He that believeth on the Son hath life.' We speak of the soul's condition as fallen, depraved, full of enmity to God. We speak of the new birth, and the gracious Spirit who works the change. We speak of the symptoms of the change, *viz.*, the sense of the serpent-bites leading the eye of the sinner toward the brazen serpent (verses 14-15),

and the heart finally inclined toward Jesus, as surely as the new-born child inclines to the mother's breast. We tell that all who ever entered rest entered by this one door. We tell them that if they have not life, then they have never believed.

5. We refer to the *sickness*. It necessarily empties the soul of the things of earth: the sick cannot enjoy them. It also gives leisure to the conscience to speak. Besides, it cries, 'Zaccheus, *make haste, make haste!*'

4

THE SICK PERSON'S SPIRITUAL STATE
IS UNKNOWN TO YOU

John 3:3, 35-36. 'Verily, verily, I say unto you, Except a man be born again, he cannot see the kingdom of God . . . The Father loveth the Son, and hath given all things into his hand. He that believeth on the Son hath everlasting life; and he that believeth not the Son shall not see life; but the wrath of God abideth upon him.'

Job 5:17-18. 'Behold, happy is the man whom God correcteth; therefore, despise not thou the chastening of the Almighty. For he maketh sore and bindeth up; he woundeth, and his hands make whole.'

> This trouble may have blessed results. Sickness is some men's tide-time. 1. It may be God is taking you aside that you may learn well some of his solemn lessons. 2. Do not think that this dealing is one which you may overlook. 3. It is God only who can heal soul and body. He set up

the serpent of brass for the bitten ones in the camp of Israel, and he has lifted up his own Son on the cross for the sin-bitten soul.

Hos. 7:14. 'They have not cried unto me with their hearts, when they howled upon their beds.'

> Like Absalom setting fire to Joab's fields of corn in order to ensure a visit from Joab, who would not fail to come and ask what all this meant—so, their trouble is sent to cause them to go and speak with the Lord. God is waiting to see the result.

Lam. 3:40-41. 'Let us search and try our ways, and turn again to the Lord. Let us lift up our heart with our hands unto God in the heavens.'

> 1. Searching into self will discover to ourselves that we are sinners; one sin after another will come to light, like as the digging in the rubbish of Nineveh casts up continually new remains. 2. Convinced of sin, no course is left us but *'turning to God'*, *i.e.* repairing to him for the pardon he has promised, and for all the blessings that follow upon that pardon. By nature, the sinner's *face* is toward the world, and his *back* on the law and on God. In conversion, his face is turned toward the law and toward the law-fulfilling Saviour.

Luke 15:18, 20. 'I will arise and go to my father . . . And he arose and came to his father. But when he was yet a great way off, his father saw him, and had compassion, and ran and fell upon his neck and kissed him.'

> The prodigal's reception *depended on what the father was,* not on what he himself was. He was restored not because he deserved it, but because the father *delighted to pour out free love.*

Rom. 5:12, 15. 'By one man sin entered into the world, and death by sin; and so death passed upon all men, for that all have sinned . . . But not as the offence, so also is the free gift. For, if through the offence of one, many be dead, much more the grace of God and the gift by grace, which is by one man, Jesus Christ, hath abounded unto many.'

> 1. When one is sick, death stands over him and shakes his dart. The sick one is reminded thereby of his being a sinner, one of fallen Adam's family. 2. But let him also remember the second Adam, who lifts up the fallen; and see him full of grace, the channel of God's free love, and of the gift of life to sinners.

Ezek. 18:4, 20. 'The soul that sinneth, it shall die . . . The soul that sinneth, it shall die.'

Isa. 55:3. 'Hear, and your soul shall live.'

> Dying sinner, the Holy Spirit, who convinceth thee of sin, also showeth thee eternal life in Jesus. 1. Did the testimony of God to thy sinfulness strike dead thy hopes of saving thyself? Then, let the testimony of God concerning his Son convey life to thee. 2. Life comes to you when you are believing the good news that Jesus Christ 'poured out his soul unto death' (*Isa.* 53:12), 'made his soul an offering for sin' (*Isa.* 53:10), pleasing the Lord by his being thus

bruised for sin. *Hear this;* is it not good tidings?

Eccles. 1:2. 'Vanity of vanities, saith the preacher, vanity of vanities; all is vanity!'

> If sickness does no more, at least it empties thee of earth. It bales out the waters from all thy broken cisterns.

Song of Sol. 1:1-2. 'The Song of Songs, which is Solomon's. Let him kiss me with the kisses of his mouth, for thy love is better than wine.'

> Emptied of the world, here is an object to fill thy soul, *viz.*, he of whom Solomon sings, The Lord Jesus Christ; at whose voice they who know him leap for joy.

John 1:29. 'Behold the Lamb of God, that taketh away the sin of the world.'

Luke 19:5, 10. 'Zaccheus, make haste and come down, for to-day I must abide at thy house . . . For the Son of man is come to seek and to save that which was lost.'

Acts 5:31. 'Him hath God exalted by his right hand to be a Prince and Saviour, to give repentance to Israel and forgiveness of sins . . . And we are his witnesses of these things.'

> Even Israel may get these gifts! The most guilty, the most unbelieving, the most self-righteous, may find him waiting to show mercy.

2 Sam. 14:14. 'For we must needs die, and are as water spilt on the ground, which cannot be gathered up again;

neither doth God respect any person: yet doth he devise means that his banished be not expelled from him.'

> Here we are reminded that—1. We have only one life. 2. The end of that life is sure. 3. God is strictly just, and not a judge that can be bribed to do evil. 4. Yet, nevertheless, God provided cities of refuge for the manslayer, with the view of saving his life, and bringing him afterwards home again. 5. In this we see a type of our spiritual case. Think of our one life only—of a coming eternity—of God the judge so holy; and haste thee to the provision he has made, in consistency with justice, for the escape of thy soul.

Job 35:9-10. 'By reason of the multitude of oppressions, they make the oppressed to cry; they cry out by reason of the arm of the mighty. But none saith, Where is God my Maker, who giveth songs in the night!'

> 'We have as much need of God's blessing with the rod, as with our daily bread.'—*Caryl*.

Psa. 119:18-19. 'Open thou mine eyes, that I may behold wondrous things out of thy law. I am a stranger in the earth, hide not thy commandments from me.'

Psa. 84:47. 'Remember how short my time is!'

Psa. 39:12-13. 'I am a stranger with thee and a sojourner, as all my fathers were. O spare me, that I may recover strength before I go hence and be no more.'

> 1. The 'sparing' means here, as in Mal. 3:17, God, in sovereign grace, forbearing to inflict deserved wrath. 2. It is this

grace of God that restores spiritual strength to the soul, and enables it to go on its journey to the mount of God.

Heb. 2:3. 'How shall we escape if we neglect so great salvation?'

Heb. 4:1. 'Let us, therefore, fear lest, a promise being left us of entering into his rest, any of you should seem to come short of it.'

> As if he had said: 'Be so decidedly like Caleb and Joshua, that you shall never once be mistaken by any for persons who agreed with the unbelieving Israelites, whose hearts yielded to the evil report of the ten spies.'

Heb. 3:19. 'So we see that they could not enter in because of unbelief'!

Heb. 9:27. 'It is appointed unto men once to die; but after this the judgment.'

Amos 5:4, 6, 8-9. 'Seek ye me, and ye shall live . . . Seek the Lord, and ye shall live . . . Seek him that maketh the seven stars and Orion, and turneth the shadow of death into the morning, and maketh the day dark with night: that calleth for the waters of the sea, and poureth them out upon the face of the earth: the Lord is his name: that strengtheneth the spoiled against the strong . . . Seek good and not evil [verse 14] that ye may live; and so the Lord God of Hosts shall be with you.'

Matt. 9:2. 'And, behold, they brought to him a man sick of the palsy, lying on a bed: and Jesus, seeing their faith, said unto the sick of the palsy, Son, be of good cheer; thy sins be forgiven thee.'

> 1: Here are friends approved of by Christ for bringing to him their sick. He has respect to *their* faith, as well as to the sick man's. 2. Here we are taught that pardon of sin is better than health of body. It is a pillow for a weary head. 3. Here we are taught to seek this pardon first; health may then follow, as in verse 6.

Introduction to Chapter 5

The Sick Person Lacks Knowledge

WE need with us that same Holy Spirit who said to Philip, 'Go near and join thyself to this chariot' (*Acts* 8:29), and who stood by him as he opened up to the Ethiopian eunuch the way of salvation through the Lamb led to the slaughter. That man was very ignorant (verses 31-34); he confessed that what he read was altogether dark to him, yet Philip went to him. And was it vain? Did not the man 'go on his way rejoicing'? You may have to deal with one as ignorant, or one who, though he knows the letter, does not know the spirit of the Word. The Lord may use you as he did Philip. Go on; speak calmly, kindly, plainly; patiently, too.

1. Perhaps you take up 1 Tim. 2:4, 'God our Saviour, who will have all men to be saved, and to come unto the knowledge of the truth.' *a.* You tell the person that, just

as the Lord in ancient days appointed cities of refuge, and would have all who were unwittingly manslayers to flee thereto: so is it in regard to their souls. *b.* You speak of God's compassion for souls, and declare that the sinner's death is not to be laid to God's charge, but at the door of sin. *c.* You show that, desirous as God is to save, he saves none who do not know and receive that Saviour who is 'the Way, the Truth, and the Life'.

Or you take up Psa. 9:10, 'They that know thy name will put their trust in thee.' You show that it is *want of acquaintance with God* that lies at the root of *want of faith*. You show, too, how they who know him love him, being drawn irresistibly to him. And so you seek to excite interest and awake desire.

2. Perhaps you need here again to give a caution regarding James 5:16, noticed in the introduction to the former chapter. On the same account, also, it is most necessary in the case of the ignorant, not to indulge their idea of its being the main duty of the visitor to *pray with* them. It may often be advisable to go away without praying *with* them, if you see any tendency to this abuse. You can pray *for* them alone.

3. Rousing words and plain explanations of the truth should go together in this case. Such texts as are suggested

here may furnish matter of this sort; but they must be accompanied with patient and persevering teaching. Remember our Lord's patience with Nicodemus and with the woman of Samaria.

5

THE SICK PERSON
LACKS KNOWLEDGE

1 **Tim. 2:4.** 'God our Saviour, who will have all men to be saved, and to come unto the knowledge of the truth.'

> N.B. — *No salvation without the knowledge of him that saves.*

John 4:10. 'Jesus answered and said unto her, If thou knewest the gift of God, and who it is that saith unto thee, Give me to drink; thou wouldest have asked of him, and he would have given thee living water.'

> Ignorance of God's generous and liberal gift of life, and of him who is the means of bringing it to us, Jesus his Son, hinders men from even thirsting for the water of life.

1 **John 4:16.** 'We have known and believed the love that God hath to us.'

We must *know* it first, and then there is material for faith.

Luke 6:39. 'If the blind lead the blind, both shall fall into the ditch.'

Prov. 14:12. 'There is a way that seemeth right unto a man, but the end thereof are the ways of death.' The same truth is asserted again in chap. 16:25.

Luke 19:42. 'If thou hadst known, even thou, at least in this thy day the things which belong unto thy peace.'

Prov. 29:18. 'Where there is no vision, the people perish.'[1]

2 Cor. 4:3. 'But if our gospel be hid, it is hid to them that are lost.'

> If there be not a spiritual knowledge of the gospel, the soul is lost. Of course, then, it cannot be saved while not knowing it even doctrinally.

Acts 3:17, 19. 'And now, brethren, I wot that through ignorance ye did it, as did also your rulers . . . Repent ye, therefore, and be converted.'

---

[1] 'In a shower of rain, you would not turn aside into a shelter unless you knew that there was a shelter there. Though you had lived at the time of the flood, if you had lived in complete ignorance of the ark, you would not have fled to it. Or even if you had known it, and seen it, and heard of it, yet if you did not know the use of it, you would never have fled to it. So it is with sinners now. Many do not know about Jesus. Many know something about him, but they do not know the use of him to their perishing souls, and so they will not come to him and have life. Do not say you are too old to learn. If the Spirit be your teacher, he can make it easy.—*M'Cheyne.*

Hos. 4:6. 'My people are destroyed for lack of knowledge. Because thou hast rejected knowledge, I also will reject thee.'

Acts 8:30-31, 35. 'Understandest thou what thou readest? And he said, How can I, except some one should guide me? And he desired Philip that he would come up and sit with him . . . Then Philip opened his mouth, and began at the same Scripture, and preached unto him Jesus.'

> This inquiring soul was not saved until he was made to know the sense of what he read, and then to know the doctrine it conveyed. The Holy Spirit uses *knowledge of Christ* as his instrument in saving.

Isa. 53:11. 'By his knowledge, shall my righteous servant justify many' [*i.e.* These many shall discover, by knowing him, how God justifies the sinner].

Heb. 11:6. 'He that cometh unto God must believe that he is, and that he is a rewarder of them that diligently seek him.'

> 1. In coming to God, we must know his real nature, his character, his perfections; otherwise, we come to an unknown God. 2. We must know him as the God who delights to reward with eternal life all who come by faith, *i.e.* all who come believing *what he is in his Son*. 3. They who 'diligently seek' are they who never cease their search till they find him. They *'seek him out'*.

Psa. 9:10. 'They that know thy name, will put their trust in thee.'

John 14:5-6. 'Lord, we know not whither thou goest, and how can we know the way? Jesus saith unto him, I am the way, and the truth, and the life: No man cometh unto the Father but by me. If ye had known me, ye should have known my Father also.'

1 Cor. 2:11-12. 'The things of God knoweth no man (no one), but the Spirit of God. Now we have received not the spirit of the world, but the Spirit that is of God, that we might know the things that are freely given us of God.'

> This is more than head-knowledge; but yet it cannot exist in the absence of head-knowledge. The Spirit must give the true heart acquaintance with saving truth; but the materials must be there previously. Jesus turned into wine only as much water as was in the six vessels of stone.—John 2:7. When no more vessels were brought, no more oil came.—2 Kings 4:6.

Lev. 4:27. 'And if any one of the common people sin through ignorance, while he doeth somewhat against any of the commandments of the Lord, concerning things which ought not to be done, and be guilty; or if his sin which he has sinned, come to his knowledge; then he shall bring his offering, a kid of the goats, a female without blemish, for his sin which he hath sinned.'

> 1. Ignorance saves no man from guilt. 2. Ignorance may be heaping up sin. 3. We ought to repent of times of ignorance;

they were times of sin. 4. The man who has been ignorant and so has been sinning, though unthinkingly, must flee to the sacrifice.

2 Pet. 1:2. 'Grace and peace be multiplied unto you through the knowledge of God, and of Jesus our Lord.'

Jesus at Jacob's Well

Jesus, to what didst thou submit
To save thy dear-bought flock from hell!
Like a poor traveller see him sit,
Athirst and weary by the well.

The woman who for water came
(What great events on small depend!)
Then learnt the glory of his name,—
The Well of life, the Sinner's Friend.

Taught from her birth to hate the Jews,
And filled with party-pride, at first
Her zeal induced her to refuse
Water to quench the Saviour's thirst.

But soon she knew the gift of God;
And Jesus whom she scorned before,
Unasked, that drink on her bestowed,
Which whoso tastes shall thirst no more.

His words her prejudice removed;
Her sin she felt, relief she found;
She saw and heard—believed and lived,
And ran to tell her neighbours round.

The Sick Person lacks Knowledge

'O come, this wondrous man behold—
The promised Saviour! This is he
Whom ancient prophecies foretold,
Born from our guilt to set us free.'

Like her in ignorance content,
I worshipped long I knew not what;
Like her, on other things intent,
He found me when I sought him not.

He told me all that e'er I did:
And told me all was pardoned too!
And now, like her, as He has bid,
I live to point Him out to you.

John Newton.

Introduction to Chapter 6

The Sick Person Is Self-righteous

THE Holy Spirit's office and delight is to 'glorify Christ' (*John* 16:14). It is he who must be with us when we deal with the self-righteous, 'casting down imaginations and every high thing that exalteth itself against the knowledge of God'. O pray for his presence.

1. It may be well to ask the person to state the scheme of salvation to you.

2. It may be well to put questions, and by these probe the conscience.

3. It would be most desirable to ascertain the phase, or form, of self-righteousness with which you have to deal. Is the man trusting in decency of character? in integrity?

in amiability? Is he resting on church attendance, sacraments, prayer?—Is he making a Saviour out of his own efforts and earnestness? Is he fancying that his sorrow, repentance, convictions, joined perhaps with his love, will recommend him to God? Is he making *faith itself* his Saviour? It may be, he is resting (as John Berridge did so long) *partly* on the rock, *partly* on the sand; partly on the sound plank, partly on the rotten; partly on a Christ, and partly on supposed Christian graces!

4. Suppose we take up Hag. 1:7, '*Consider your ways.*'

We ask the person to review his case fearlessly, anxiously. There is no time to lose, and the result of error will be *eternal death!* We then make such suggestions as those stated above. We go on to state the one only Righteousness for sinners.

Or we take up Isa. 59:6, 'Their web shall not become garments, neither shall they cover themselves with their works.' We show that many serious and thoughtful souls are making webs out of *their own works*. We show, therefore, that *nothing* made out of *our doing* will please God; it is no better than Adam's fig-leaves. Works, or prayers, or services of fifty years' standing will not do. We then, perhaps, take up such a chapter as Rom. 4 or Rom. 10, to exhibit the real righteousness; or we dwell upon such an expression as Rom. 3:21, *'the righteousness of God without the law'*. Or we open out the meaning of *'the Lord our Righteousness'*. or we stay upon Rom. 10:4.

5. Let us keep our own soul on edge as well as alarm those we have to do with, by such a thought as this, 'How dreadful the fall from the high turret of presumption into the deep pit of perdition!'—*Swinnock*.

6

THE SICK PERSON IS SELF-RIGHTEOUS

Hag. 1:7. 'Thus saith the Lord of Hosts, Consider your ways.'

Isa. 59:6. 'Their webs shall not become garments; neither shall they cover themselves with their works.'

Jer. 9:23, 25. 'Thus saith the Lord, Let not the wise man glory in his wisdom, neither let the mighty man glory in his might; let not the rich man glory in his riches. But let him that glorieth, glory in this, that he understandeth and knoweth me, that I am the Lord which exercise loving-kindness, judgment, and righteousness in the earth; for in these things I delight, saith the Lord.'

> 1. Have you ceased to glory in whatever is yours? 2. Do you glory in the Lord as alone worthy to be spoken of and thought upon? 3. Do you see matter for glorying in his *righteousness,* as well as his mercy? in his holy rules of judgment, as well as in his loving-kindness?

Jer. 17:5, 7. 'Thus saith the Lord, Cursed be the man that trusteth in man, and maketh flesh his arm, and whose heart departeth from the Lord . . . Blessed is the man that trusteth in the Lord, and whose hope the Lord is.'

> If you are a dying man, consider this as the only time left you for eternity. If you are leaning on what is not divine, the moment you die you shall find out your delusion; for you shall be as the heath in the desert, seeing no good, but feeling the scorching heat for ever!

Matt. 22:11. 'And when the king came in to see the guests, he saw there a man which had not a wedding garment; and he saith unto him, Friend, how camest thou in hither, not having a wedding garment? And he was speechless.'

Eccles. 8:10. 'And so I saw the wicked buried, who had come and gone from the place of the holy, and they were forgotten in the city when they had so done. This is also vanity.'

> 1. You may have frequented the sanctuary; you may have sat at the Lord's table, as these in ancient days frequented the temple and altar; and yet you may be still without God. 2. You may die in this state of formality, and have funeral honours paid you. 3. But what will it avail you? You will be forgotten soon on earth; and what place will you have in the world to come?

Matt. 7:22-23. 'Many will say to me in that day, Lord, Lord, have we not prophesied in thy name? and in thy name have cast out devils? and in thy name done many wonderful works? And then I will profess unto them, I never knew you! Depart from me, ye that work iniquity.'

> Are you putting stress on your profession? on your service of him? on your gifts? on what he has enabled you to do or say? Then, you are building on the sand. You ought to have grounded all your confidence, in regard to acceptance, on *himself* alone.

Luke 13:25-26. 'Many shall seek to enter in and not be able. When once the master of the house is risen and hath shut to the door . . . then shall ye begin to say, We have eaten and drunk in thy presence, and thou hast taught[1] in our streets.'

Jer. 6:14. 'They have healed also the hurt of the daughter of my people slightly, saying, Peace, peace, when there is no peace.'

> The fall broke off man's communion with God. All sin and every sin sets a gulf between our souls and God. This is 'the hurt'. The healing of the hurt, therefore, must be a restoring of us to *fellowship with God*. Such peace with God is not simply a quiet conscience. It is far more than silence after storm. It is the universal movement of the soul, freed from guilt and fear, toward God in whom it delights.

Ezek. 13:10, 13. 'Because, even because, they have seduced my people, saying, "Peace", and there is no peace;

---

[1] 'I may be a book-man, and at the best a fool, in Christ's way. The Bible beguiled the Pharisees, and so may I be misled.'—*S. Rutherford.*

and one built up a wall, and others daubed it with un-tempered mortar . . . Therefore thus saith the Lord God, I will even rend it with a stormy wind in my fury, and there shall be an overflowing shower in mine anger, and great hailstones in my fury to consume it.'

Mark 10:20-22. 'Master, all these have I observed from my youth. Then Jesus beholding him, loved him and said unto him, One thing thou lackest; go thy way, sell whatsoever thou hast, and give to the poor (and thou shalt have treasure in heaven); and come, take up the cross, and follow me. And he was sad at that saying, and went away grieved.'

> 1. Jesus sees glaring deficiency in obedience which we fancy to be faultless. 2. It was love to that soul which led him to probe the sore, and cause the corruption to ooze out. 3. Whatever else we do, one thing remains for us as the only remedy for our case *'Follow me'*. We must let Jesus lead us to his own finished work.

Rom. 10:3-4. 'They being ignorant of God's righteous-ness [i.e. *the righteousness required, and provided for us, by God in the person and the work of Messiah*], and go-ing about to establish their own righteousness, have not submitted themselves unto the righteousness of God. For Christ is the end of the law for righteousness to everyone that believeth.'

> 1. What Christ, God-man, has done is exactly what the law

sought from men. He is the only one in our nature that has accomplished this. 2. He has accomplished it altogether for the sake of others, not for himself. 3. Whoever knows and believes this has found out a mine of wealth, riches of righteousness! 4. Will you now cease from efforts at weaving a web of your own? Will you 'submit' to receive this wrought robe, of divine and human workmanship?

John 6:28-29. 'What shall we do to work the works of God? Jesus answered and said unto them, This is the work of God, that ye believe in him whom he has sent.'

> Instead of saying that your paltry, polluted services please a holy God, he tells you that he would fain see you ceasing from such self-gratifying deeds, and looking, gazing, poring over the perfect, spotless, completely satisfying work of Jesus, whom the Father sent to do the work which we all fail to do.

Luke 1:53. 'He hath filled the hungry with good things, but the rich he hath sent empty away.'

Isa. 55:1. 'Ho! every one that thirsteth, come ye to the waters, and he that hath no money, come ye, buy and eat; yea, come, buy wine and milk, without money and without price.'

> 1. Even suppose there were a price put on salvation-blessings, *you* are not to give it; come 'without money'. But they are not priced at all; they are beyond price, and bestowed as gifts without one single quality on your part deserving the gift. 2. Yet *'buy'* all this—make it as surely *yours as if you had paid the whole price* at which it was worth. *'Buy'*

it; make it your own so fully that law itself will defend you in possession of it. 3. And all this '*buying*' is just your soul receiving, making welcome, or really believing, God's report concerning the Saviour, and the Saviour's doing and dying. See Isa. 53.

Rev. 3:17-18. 'Thou sayest, I am rich, and increased with goods, and have need of nothing: and knowest not that thou art wretched and miserable [*q.d.* a miserable wretch], and poor and blind [*q.d.* a blind beggar], and naked. I counsel thee to buy of me gold tried in the fire that thou mayest be rich: and white raiment that thou mayest be clothed, and the shame of thy nakedness do not appear; and anoint thine eyes with eye-salve that thou mayest see.'

> '*Buy*' is the same sense as Isa. 55:1. Buy, 1. The ransom money. 2. The dress for the presence of the king. 3. The Spirit who shows thee all that a sinner's eye may be satisfied in seeing. *N.B.* — Nothing removes nakedness, poverty, blindness, but what is got from Christ.[2]

Hos. 12:8. 'And Ephraim said, Yet I am become rich, I

---

[2] Cecil (on visiting death-beds) proposes, that, in speaking to others, we should sometimes begin with ourselves. It disarms pride, conciliates attention, and may insinuate conviction. Thus: 'Whatever others think of themselves, I stand condemned before God; my heart is so "*desperately wicked*", that if God had not showed me in his Word a remedy in Jesus Christ, I should be in despair. I can only tell you what I am and what I have found. If *you* believe yourselves to be what God has told me *I am*, and all men are, then I can tell you where and how to find mercy and eternal life. If you will not believe that you are *this sort of man*, I have nothing to offer you.'

have found me out substance. In all my labours they shall find no iniquity in me that were sin!'

> 'Here is poison! To set the law in room of the Mediator.'
> —*Bunyan*.

Jer. 2:23. 'How canst thou say, I am not polluted, I have not gone after Baalim! See thy way in the valley; know what thou hast done!'

Hos. 14:3. 'In thee the fatherless findeth mercy.'

Isa. 1:14. 'Your new moons and your appointed feasts, my soul hateth. They are a trouble unto me; I am weary to bear them.'

> The person must first be accepted; then the performance. First Abel, then his offering (*Gen.* 4:4.); for Abel's faith covered him with Jesus Christ.' —*Bunyan*.

1 John 4:8. 'Herein is love! Not that we loved God, but that he loved us, and sent his Son to be the propitiation for our sins.'

John 15:16. 'Ye have not chosen me, but I have chosen you.'

Rom. 9:16. 'So then, it is not of him that willeth, nor of him that runneth, but of God that sheweth mercy.'

> No man can glory in self; for, if now he be willing, it was God that changed his will and made him so; and if now he run in the way, he has to thank God who set him on his feet and gave him power to run. Salvation in its beginning, and at every stage, is 'of God who sheweth mercy'.

John 19:30. 'It is finished.'

> Have you felt the power there is in these words to give peace? For soon the cry, *'It is done'* (*Rev.* 21:6), will end all hope of change.

Phil. 3:8-9. 'I count all things but loss for the excellency of the knowledge of Christ Jesus, my Lord! . . . I do count them [even my great advantages and personal qualities] but dung, that I may win Christ; and be found in him, not having mine own righteousness, which is of the law, but that which is through the faith of Christ, the righteousness which is of God [provided by God] by faith [made ours by faith).'

> 1. Being found thus clothed, when the Lord calls us away, or when the Lord comes again, we shall like Paul have part (verses 10-11) in the Resurrection of the Just, knowing Christ, the power of his resurrection, the fellowship of his sufferings, and being made conformable to his death.
> 2. To be ever seeking to *'win Christ'*, *i.e.* gain more and more out of that mine of wealth, is one great help against self-righteousness.

INTRODUCTION TO CHAPTER 7

THE SICK PERSON IS ANXIOUS

WE have as much need of the Holy Spirit with us, in trying to impart light to a soul sensible of its darkness, as in seeking to awaken the dead. For who but God can command light to shine into their hearts? This also cometh from the Lord of Hosts. 'As many as believe in his name', were born, 'not of blood, nor of the will of the flesh, nor of the will of man, but of God' (*John* 1:13). It is the Spirit who 'reproves the world of righteousness' (*John* 16:8).

It is good, in an easy way, to question the person who seems anxious, and thus if possible to draw out the real state of his mind. It is better still when, unprompted, the person is ready to ask questions at us.

At all events, let us ascertain the real state of his mind, and not shoot an arrow at a venture. Thus we read:—

1. Luke 3:10, 12, 14, where the question is thrice put, *'What shall we do?'* the meaning being, What is our way of proving our repentance to be genuine? The people, the publicans, and the soldiers, each got a distinct and different reply from the Baptist on that occasion, because they were asking about something else than the one way of salvation. They were asking about each man's special way of glorifying God in his daily life.

2. We read the young ruler's question, Mark 10:17, 'What shall I do that I may inherit eternal life?' What reply shall we give to that? We must understand his state of mind: and, discerning rightly what is his state, must deal accordingly. We cannot, like our Master, see into souls; and, therefore, we put questions to elicit information. And if we find the man is, like the young ruler, one who fancies he could *save himself* if only he were rightly directed what to do, we seek to drive this idea out of his mind. Often one may use illustrations, or suggest circumstances, which may flash into his mind the conviction of the impossibility of his bringing himself out of the forest in which he has lost his way.

3. We find others really in the state of the Philippian jailor (*Acts* 16:30). Their very words, as well as tone, tell their deep anxiety: 'What MUST I do?' and they have not

committed themselves to any false plan. They are seeking to see the one only true way. These we at once address as Paul and Silas did. The way to be saved is, *Believing in one who has done all salvation-work already*—believing in Christ who has done it in his own person, for our sakes, and in our name.

There is no need of being afraid, as some are, to tell the anxious that it is the Holy Spirit who shows Christ to the soul. This will hinder none. There is no need of being afraid that, if we tell them that God has chosen whom he will to eternal life, they will be hindered thereby. At the same time, the great truth we have to deal with in their circumstances, is this, that 'Christ once suffered for sins, the just for the unjust, to bring us unto God.'

7

THE SICK PERSON IS ANXIOUS

John 12:35-36. 'Yet a little while is the light with you . . . While ye have light, believe in the light, that ye may be children of light.'

Psa. 30:9. 'What profit is there in my blood when I go down to the pit? shall the dust praise thee, shall it declare thy truth?'

Matt. 11:25-26. 'I thank thee, O Father, Lord of heaven and earth, because thou hast hid these things from the wise and prudent, and hast revealed them unto babes. Even so, Father, for so it seemed good in thy sight.'

> 1. Christ delighted to call to mind his Father's sovereignty. Specially notice that he prefaces his call to sinners (verse 28) with it; for it assures us that there is no case hopeless if the Lord choose. He can open the blindest eye; he can soften the hardest heart; he can pardon the vilest of the vile, the basest of men. 2. Salvation consists not in a great amount of knowledge, nor in the exercise of great intellect.

For see, a very babe (in years or in understanding) can be made truly to comprehend 'these things'. Salvation is found by him who sees Christ to be *the sinner's Saviour*—even though he know as little else as did *'Poor Joseph'*.

Matt. 11:28. 'Come unto me, all ye that labour and are heavy laden, and I will give you rest.'

After proclaiming himself (verse 27) fully furnished by the Father to save—as being the world's Joseph, who had stores of corn for the famishing—he here invites men. 1. He invites sinners, for these are the *'heavy-laden'*. Whether they feel their load or not, he invites them, for they are laden, and they need him. 2. He invites *'labouring'* sinners, those who are trying to save themselves, those who are weary in the attempt to find salvation, 3. He invites them to *himself*—not to duties, sacraments, prayers, the Bible, doctrines, not even to faith, apart from the *object* of faith. 4. There is no stress to be laid on the 'come', as if it were a difficult act of the soul. It is here a particle that means: *'This way! this way! to me!'* Let your soul leave self out of its thoughts, and every thing and person but *Christ* alone. 5. This is rest. You are done with travelling now. 6. It is *after you have come to him,* that he adds (verse 30), 'Take my yoke', *i.e.* now go forth and serve me. After (but not till after) you have found him, you are to work. And then you get a second 'rest', namely, that of holiness, becoming 'meek and lowly', the sea of passion calmed.

Gal. 1:16. 'It pleased God . . . to reveal his Son in me.'

Heb. 5:2. 'Who can have compassion on the ignorant,

and on them that are out of the way.' Compare Deut. 22:1. 'Thou shalt not see thy brother's ox or sheep go astray and hide thyself from them'; (But how much is a man better than a sheep or ox? and Jesus more ready to help than any neighbour?)

Psa. 43:3. 'O send forth thy light and thy truth, let them lead me. Let them bring me unto thy holy hill, and to thy tabernacles. Then will I go unto the altar of God.'

Psa. 143:10. 'Thy Spirit is good; lead me to the land of uprightness.'

John 7:37. 'If any man thirst, let him come unto me and drink.'

> 1. The *thirsty* man is the soul that feels *unsatisfied* whether more or less sensible of sin, it matters not to the welcome conveyed by this invitation. 2. The *object* that will *satisfy* that soul is *Christ*.

John 5:44. 'How can ye believe who seek honour one of another, and seek not the honour that cometh from God only.'

> Deal simply with God—not with men's opinions. Neither seek the smile, nor fear the frown of man; seek only the good-will of God in his Son.

Luke 2:10. 'Fear not,[1] for behold I bring you good tidings of great joy . . . unto you is born this day in the city

---

[1] 'Thy fear may arise from thine own folly in chalking out to God a way to bring thee home to Christ.'—*Bunyan*.

of David, a Saviour, which is Christ the Lord.'

> 1. You are not to be left to do your best. 2. You are not to be bidden help yourself out of the pit. 3. You are not to be shown a way of helping yourself out. 4. You are not to be asked to do or suffer, in body or mind, any one thing in order to your pardon and peace. 5. Behold! *Christ does all for you;* all that brings pardon and peace is done by him. Believest thou this? Wilt thou let him draw thee out of the pit with his own hands?

1 Pet. 2:2. 'As new-born babes, receive the sincere milk of the word.'

Luke 24:25. 'O fools, and slow of heart to believe all that the prophets have spoken.'

Psa. 95:7. 'Today, if ye will hear his voice.' Heb. 3:7. 'Today.' Heb. 4:7. 'Today.'

Isa. 53:5. 'The chastisement of our peace was laid on him; and by his stripes we are healed.'

> 'We carve out religion for ourselves, and make it ten times more difficult than the Bible makes it', says one. It is not by our own stripes, nor yet by our own strivings, but by Christ's chastisement and stripes, that healing comes.

Psa. 84:9. 'O God, behold our shield. Look upon the face of thine anointed.'

> God looks on Jesus at his right hand, and is satisfied. But are you content merely with praying thus? Do you look as well as pray? Look yourself, as well as ask God to look, on the face of Christ.

Psa. 35:3. 'Say to my soul, I am thy salvation.'

Psa. 70:5. 'But I am poor and needy, make haste unto me, O God.'

> Let the storm hasten thy escape, O dove, to the clefts of the rock.

Judg. 10:15. 'His soul was grieved for the misery of Israel.'

Mic. 6:8. 'He hath shewn thee, O man, what is good.'

> The man had asked, 'Wherewith shall I come before the Lord.' The answer says, 'He hath shewn thee.' Go to the altar—go to Calvary—and see. He has shown thee *Christ's* doing and dying. Believe that as thy warrant for going before the Lord; and AFTER that, 'Do justly, love mercy, and walk humbly with thy God.'[2]

Mic. 7:18. 'Who is a God like unto thee, that pardoneth iniquity, and passeth by the transgression of the remnant of his heritage? He retaineth not his anger for ever, because he delighteth in mercy. He will return again; he will have compassion upon us.'

2 Cor. 6:2. 'Behold, now is the accepted time. Behold, now is the day of salvation.'

> So long as Christ presents his offered sacrifice to the Father as sufficient, even so long does the day of grace last. Now, therefore, now, look at that all-sufficient sacrifice and live.

---

[2] 'If you should believe or doubt for your goodness' sake which you feel or feel not, then should you make Christ Jesus to you nothing, or else but half Christ.'—*Bradford.*

Heb. 7:25. 'Therefore he is able also to save them to the uttermost that come unto God BY HIM, seeing he ever liveth to make intercession for them.'

Mark 5:36. 'Daughter, thy faith hath made thee whole.'

> She had done no more than tremblingly touch only the tassel of his robe. So there was no merit in *the act itself*. On the other hand, she was led to give that touch from *believing Jesus to be full to the brim* with healing virtue. This was faith. 'Remember', says one, 'it is not by grace *within* you, but by free grace *without you,* that you are to be saved.'

Rev. 22:17. 'Whosoever will let him come, and let him take the water of life freely.'

> One of the last words spoken by Jesus from heaven, addressed to all who may ever hear or read them. *N.B.*—He says 'FREELY', *i.e.* it is bestowed without regard to anything in you, done by you, felt by you, spoken by you, possessed by you. It is done in the absence of every claim on your part.

2 Chron. 15:4. 'When they in their trouble did turn unto the Lord God of Israel and sought him, he was found of them.'

Isa. 25:4. 'Thou hast been a strength to the poor, a strength to the needy in his distress; a refuge for the storm, a shadow from the heat.'

Isa. 12:2-3. 'Behold, God is my salvation; I will trust and not be afraid, for the Lord Jehovah is my strength and my song; he also is become my salvation. Therefore with joy shall ye draw water out of the wells of salvation.'[3]

> Understanding *'the wells of salvation'* to be the same as *'the waters'* in chap. 55:1,—notice, 1. Your warrant to approach and draw is *nothing in yourself*. 2. It is this:—'The *Lord Jehovah* is my salvation': inasmuch as the Lord Jesus furnishes the obedience and the suffering due, all that makes justice refuse to allow of mercy's approach to the sinner. 3. Thinking on this, may you not joyfully say, 'Herein my thirsty soul has found the wells of salvation'?

Psa. 23:1, 3. 'The Lord is my shepherd. He leadeth me in the paths of righteousness, for his name's sake.'

> To show what he himself is (*viz.*, gracious, and able, through the Sacrifice, to justify the sinner), the Lord leadeth me in paths of righteousness. He does not do it for my sake.

Isa. 43:25. 'I, even I [whom *thou hast so rebelled against*], am he that blotteth out thy transgressions, for mine own sake, and will not remember thy sins.'

Isa. 48:9. 'For my name's sake will I defer mine anger.'

Jer. 14:21. 'Do not disgrace the throne of thy glory.'

> It is *q.d.* Do not let an evil report be brought up against thy throne, as if he that sat there had forgotten to be gra-

---

[3] 'I am sure it is sin not to eat and drink, when he saith, "Eat, O friends, drink, yea drink abundantly, O beloved.'—*S. Rutherford.*

cious. Do not let it be said that he who sits now at the right hand is not worthy to obtain for us wisdom, righteousness, sanctification and redemption. 'If there were two ways to heaven (God might say) I would not wonder that yonder people stand musing and consulting a twelvemonth. But when there is but one way, and yet people stand moping, it is this that angers God.' — *Craddock*.

Acts 10:43. 'To him give all the prophets witness, that through his name whosoever believeth in him shall receive remission of sins.'

INTRODUCTION TO CHAPTER 8

THE SICK PERSON IS A BACKSLIDER

HE alone who awoke the soul at first can awake it again. As you go to visit the backslider, cry, 'Lord, take not thy Holy Spirit from him. Restore to him the joy of thy salvation.' (*Psa.* 51:11.) Thus praying for the Holy Spirit, you go like the shipmaster in the vessel where Jonah slept, to awaken the sleeper. Remember he is ill—his time is short, perhaps. 'What meanest thou, O sleeper?'

If you take up Jeremiah 2:17, 'Hast thou not procured this unto thyself, in that thou hast forsaken the Lord thy God when he led thee by the way?' *a.* You may remind him of his lost joy, lost peace, lost days of happiness, lost love to God his Saviour. A man may tell of the loss of health; a man may tell of the loss of wealth; a man may tell of friends, influence, family, all gone, and himself left lonely; but what is this to the loss of *love and faith*? You have lost a loving heart. You have lost a believing heart. *b.* You remind him that all his sorrow and heartlessness have arisen from 'forsaking the Lord'. Absence from the fire that warms has caused his soul's coldness and numbness. *c.* You speak of the remedy. You speak of his returning to meditate again on the same truth which at first gave him rest—of meeting again (like Peter and the rest in *John* 21) the same Saviour whom he forsook. No other way, no other person, no other pardon. *d.* You encourage him by the recollections of past days. 'He led you by the way'; and how *graciously* he did it. *Not for your sake;* never was it for your worth. 'He leadeth me in the paths of righteousness, *for his own name's sake' (Psa.* 23:3), all to show the glory of his free grace.

Perhaps at another time you help him to sing, 'O for a closer walk with God', &c., or some such hymn as expresses his desires. Or, tuning David's harp, you sing Psa. 51.

You pray—it may be in the very words of Psa. 51. But you take care all the while to turn the eye of him with whom you pray to the ever-fresh, ever-new, ever-living, ever-flowing blood of Christ.

Though in one view, a backslider needs a deeper plunge into the fountain open for sin than another sinner; yet, not so in another. That is; he is as welcome as any other, he is as freely called as any other, he will as surely find the Saviour waiting for him as for any other. It is only in respect of *the backslider himself* (he being generally full of suspicions) that there are greater difficulties than in the case of any other sinner. Tell him this, and hasten his return. A dying backslider has no time to lose.

8

THE SICK PERSON IS A BACKSLIDER

1 Sam. 12:20. 'Ye have done all this wickedness; yet turn not aside from following the Lord, but serve the Lord with all your hearts.'

Jer. 2:17. 'Hast thou not procured this unto thyself, in that thou hast forsaken the Lord thy God when he led thee by the way?'

Jer. 2:19. 'Thine own wickedness shall correct thee, and thy backslidings shall reprove thee: know, therefore, and see that it is an evil thing and bitter, that thou hast forsaken the Lord thy God.'[1]

Jon. 1:3-4. 'But Jonah rose up to flee to Tarshish from the presence of the Lord . . . But the Lord sent out a great wind into the sea, and there was a mighty tempest in the sea.'

---

[1] 'An apostate has been described as the devil's prisoner broke loose, and caught by him again.'—R. *Venning*. A backslider is surely the man-slayer, who had reached the city of refuge, wandering beyond its walls within reach of the avenger.

Jon. 2:4. 'Then I said, I am cast out of thy sight. But I will look again toward thy holy temple.'

> 1. When a mighty ocean was rushing over him with its angry waves (a type of the wrath of God), and while the dark belly of the great fish (reminding him of the prison of hell) was his abode, the backslider still remembered the Lord. 2. He knew the power of *atonement,* and so speaks of the *temple* as the spot toward which he turns his eye. 3. A sinner like this can speak of the '*holy* temple', because at its altar the Holy One can meet him in peace.

Hos. 9:10. 'I found Israel like grapes in the wilderness; I saw your fathers as the first-ripe in the fig-tree at her first time. [Refreshing to the weary traveller are juicy grapes, that slake the thirst of his parched throat; and pleasant are the early figs to the husbandman; so was Israel to their God.] But they went to Baal-peor, and separated themselves to that shame.'[2]

Isa. 43:22-26. 'But thou hast not called upon me, O Jacob! But thou hast been weary of me, O Israel! Thou hast not brought me the small cattle of thy burnt-offerings, neither hast thou honoured me with thy sacrifices. I have not caused thee to serve with an offering, nor wearied thee with incense. Thou hast bought me no sweet cane with money, neither hast thou filled me with the fat of thy sac-

---

[2] Remember; 'They fall deepest into hell, who fall backward into hell. None so near heaven as those that are convinced of sin; none so near hell as those who have quenched convictions.'—*Bunyan.*

rifices; but thou hast made me to serve with thy sins; thou hast wearied me with thine iniquities. I, even I, am he that blotteth out thy transgressions, for mine own sake, and will not remember thy sins. Put me in remembrance, let us plead together: declare thou that thou mayest be justified!'

> 1. What a melancholy view of the cold-hearted, ungrateful backslider. 2. How sad and yet kind is the tone of divine regret over him! 3. Behold! what manner of grace! He ends with holding out a pardon.

Hos. 11:8-9. 'How shall I give thee up, Ephraim? How shall I deliver thee, Israel? How shall I make thee as Admah and set thee as Zeboim? Mine heart is turned within me: my repentings are kindled together. I will not execute the fierceness of my wrath; I will not return to destroy Ephraim; for I am God and not man.'

Psa. 89:30-38. 'If his children forsake my law, and walk not in my judgments; if they break my statutes and keep not my commandments; then will I visit their transgressions with the rod, and their iniquities with stripes. Nevertheless, my loving-kindness will I not utterly take from him, nor suffer my faithfulness to fail.'

> Christ, the Everlasting Father of his family, is remembered as God remembered Abraham when he destroyed Sodom, and sent forth Lot in safety. Hence his children, even when they backslide, are not cast off. They are chastised, but restored.

Rev. 2:5. 'Remember, therefore, from whence thou art fallen, and repent, and do thy first works.'

2 Chron. 12:6-7, 12. 'Whereupon the princes of Israel and the king humbled themselves; and they said, The Lord is righteous. And when the Lord saw that they humbled themselves, the word of the Lord came to Shemaiah, saying, They have humbled themselves, therefore I will not destroy them . . . When he humbled himself, the wrath of the Lord turned from him that he would not altogether destroy them. And also in Judah things went well.'

Neh. 9:28. 'When they returned and cried unto thee, thou heardest them from heaven.'

2 Sam. 12:13. 'And David said to Nathan, I have sinned against the Lord. And Nathan said unto David, The Lord also hath put away thy sin. Thou shalt not die.'

Psa. 51:2, 7-8. 'Wash me . . . cleanse me . . . purge me. Wash me and I shall be whiter than snow. Make me to hear joy and gladness, that the bones which thou hast broken may rejoice.'

1 John 1:9. 'If we confess our sins, he is faithful and just to forgive us our sins, and to cleanse us from all unrighteousness.'

1 John 1:7. 'The blood of Jesus Christ, his Son, cleanseth us from all sin.'

> Put emphasis, 1. On *the blood* of Jesus as being that of *God's Son*. The out-poured life of God-man! The life of all

that shall stand at the judgment-seat, poured out to testify the desert of sin, would not so intensely declare God's righteous determination to punish sin as the pouring out of the life of the Son of God has done. If so, it has immense value. 2. On the word *'all'*. Sin of every dye—iniquity, transgression, trespass, unrighteousness, rebellion, faults of every sort, crimes, corruptions, depravity, omissions and neglects of duty, departures from the law and love of God, backslidings of the most ungrateful character,—all this is included, for it says, 'all sin'.

Jer. 2:2. 'Go and cry in the ears of Jerusalem, saying, Thus saith the Lord, I remember thee, the kindness of thy youth, the love of thine espousals, when thou wentest after me in the wilderness, in a land that was not sown.'

That very cry intimates God's longing that you should return.

Isa. 48:18. 'O that thou hadst hearkened to my commandments! Then had thy peace been as a river, and thy righteousness as the waves of the sea.'

Isa. 55:7. 'He will abundantly pardon'; lit., 'He will multiply to pardon.'

Neh. 9:17. 'A God of pardons' (margin, Hebrew).

Luke 17:61. 'And the Lord turned and looked upon Peter. And Peter remembered the words of the Lord, how he had said unto him, Before the cock crow thou shalt deny me thrice. And Peter went out and wept bitterly.'

Compare with this the scene in John 21:15, 19, 22, not

many days after, 'Lovest thou me? Feed my sheep.' 'Follow me!' 'Follow thou me.' And so also compare Peter, the restored backslider, in his epistle (1 Pet. 2:25) writing: 'Who his own self bare our sins in his own body on the tree.' And forget not the angel's words, Mark 16:7, 'Go your way, tell his disciples, *and Peter.*'

2 Cor. 2:6, 11. 'Sufficient to such a man is this punishment, which was inflicted of many. So that contrariwise ye ought rather to forgive him and comfort him . . . Lest Satan should get an advantage of us; for we are not ignorant of his devices.'

2 Cor. 7:10. 'For godly sorrow worketh repentance unto salvation, not to be repented of; but the sorrow of the world worketh death.'

> 'Godly sorrow', is sorrow that leads the soul to God as the injured one; the man looking through his tears to God in Christ. The 'sorrow of the world', is that which leads a man to dwell chiefly and overmuch on the sadness of his condition, his disgrace, his lost influence, and such like considerations, so that the man's eye continually droops downward, never looking up to the heart of the injured Law-giver and the Law-fulfilling Saviour.

Song of Sol. 2:7. 'Many waters cannot quench love, neither can the floods drown it.'

> True most especially of God's love to us. See it in Jesus, in spite of his disciples' ignorance, folly, fear, flight, in spite of Peter's oaths, and curses, and denial. O backslider, return!

Jer. 3:22. 'Return, ye backsliding children, and I will heal your backslidings.' Ans. 'Behold we come unto thee!'

Hos. 14:4-5. 'I will heal their backslidings; I will love them freely, for mine anger is turned away from him. I will be as the dew unto Israel; he shall grow as the lily, and cast forth his roots as Lebanon. His branches shall spread.'

All this after all his backsliding!

Jer. 3:1. 'They say, if a man put away his wife, and she go from him, and become another man's, shall he return unto her again? Shall not that land [which would allow of such a thing] be greatly polluted? But thou hast played the harlot with many lovers, yet return again to me, saith the Lord!'

Grace is infinitely beyond man's conceptions; it does what man could never do, and would never do.[3]

Psa. 106:43-44. 'Many times did he deliver them, but they provoked him with their counsel, and were brought low for their iniquity. Nevertheless, he regarded their affliction, when he heard their cry: and he remembered for them his covenant and repented, according to the multitude of his mercies.'

[3] If any fear lest this should encourage carelessness or sin, let that man know, that 'the notion of free grace may make a person dissolute, but the sense of it restrains from sin.'—*Mason*. There is an invisible but indissoluble chain connecting Christ's 'Go', with his 'Sin no more.'

Hos. 2:6-7, 14. 'I will hedge up thy way with thorns, and make a wall that she shall not find her paths . . . Then shall she say, I will go and return to my first husband, for then was it better with me than now . . . I will allure her, and bring her into the wilderness, and speak comfortably to her, and I will give her her vineyards from thence [bringing her out of that wilderness to the land of vines], and the valley of Achor for a door of hope [making the valley where Israel had such trouble, the door of entrance at which she may go in with all hope]; and she shall sing there as in the days of her youth.'

> Take restored Israel's case as an emblem of yours, O backslider, in your returning to the God of grace.

INTRODUCTION TO CHAPTER 9

THE SICK PERSON IS HARDENED BECAUSE SCEPTICAL

Like David going out to battle to meet Goliath, we surely will say in this case, 'I come to thee in *the name of the Lord God* of the armies of Israel, whom thou hast defied.' We will surely call to mind that it is he who can make the pebble from the brook sink into the giant's forehead. And we will appeal to him, 'Is not thy word the *Spirit's sword!' (Eph.* 6:17). Holy Spirit, use thy word.

Remember again, John 16:8, 'When *he* is come, *he* will reprove the world of sin, of righteousness, and of judgment.'

This is the part of the sovereign Spirit; while your part is seen in Acts 24:25, 'And as Paul reasoned of righteousness, temperance, and judgment to come, Felix trembled.'

1. In a case like this, seek to win the sick one's confidence.

Approach him on the side of the affections. Be really sympathising. Take interest in his temporal matters and family; yet not officiously.

2. Do not upbraid. Patiently hear him, if he objects; patiently persevere in effort, if he is listless, and even rude.

3. Try to put yourself in his circumstances, and see how he was led to view the truth in so repulsive an aspect. And then lead him round to another view, where 'The *kindness* and *love of God to man*' appears. (*Titus* 3:4.)

4. Now, use a text. Say little in way of argument; except to silence doubt and solve real difficulties. Use *God's word*—it is *the sword*.

5. In some cases introduce a fact. For example: 'The battle's fought, the battle's fought, but the victory is lost for ever!' said one who saw truth too late; while Dr Payson could declare on his deathbed, 'The battle's fought and the victory's won! The victory is won for ever! I'm going to bathe in an ocean of purity and happiness to all eternity!'

6. Remember, the greater majority of sceptical minds are opposed to the truth because of *passion* and *feeling*,

rather than because of *principle* and *convincing argument.* Hence, we must ever use the weapons that assail *the heart* and *conscience,* whatever we ply the *head* with.

7. Never, never omit a solemn text of the word solemnly spoken in the name of the Lord.

8. Explain the way of salvation, tell of sin and the Saviour—bear testimony, whether the person hear, or whether he forbear. But do it always *tenderly* and *calmly* as in the name of the Lord.

The Missionary of Kilmany gives some striking lessons in regard to successful dealing with such persons as this chapter refers to.

9

THE SICK PERSON IS HARDENED BECAUSE SCEPTICAL

Luke 12:20. 'Thou fool, this night thy soul shall be required of thee.'

2 Pet. 1:16-19. 'For we have not followed cunningly devised fables, when we made known to you the power and coming of our Lord Jesus Christ . . . We have also a more sure word of prophecy, whereunto ye do well that ye take heed.'

Zech. 1:5-6. 'Your fathers, where are they? And the prophets, do they live for ever? But my words and my statutes, which I commanded my servants the prophets, did they not take hold of your fathers? and they returned and said, Like as the Lord of Hosts thought to do unto us, according to our ways, and according to our doings, so hath he dealt with us.'

Here we have, 1. The argument from fulfilled prophecy, or

threatening. 2. Also the solemn thought of death approaching to those living now, as it came on these of old.

John 7:17. 'If any man will do his will, he shall know of the doctrine, whether it be of God, or whether I speak of myself.'

John 3:19-20. 'And this is the condemnation, that light is come into the world, and men loved darkness rather than light, because their deeds were evil. For everyone that doeth evil hateth the light, neither cometh to the light, lest his deeds should be reproved. But he that doeth truth cometh to the light, that his deeds may be made manifest that they are wrought in God.'

Psa. 119:98, 100, 103. 'Thou, through thy commandments, hast made me wiser than my enemies . . . I understand more than the ancients, because I keep thy precepts . . . How sweet are thy words unto my taste; yea, sweeter than honey to my mouth.'

> Use the argument of personal experience; what *you* have felt, tasted, enjoyed. *You* have tried a way of happiness, which the *sceptical man* never has tried. So that you have your actual experience to bring forward against his non-experience—like a traveller telling what he has seen, to shut the mouth of those who must own they never were in that country, and so are not able to deny facts thus attested.

Eph. 2:3-5. 'Among whom we all had our conversation in times past, in the lusts of our flesh, fulfilling the desires of the flesh and of the mind; and were by nature the children of wrath even as others. But God, who is rich in mercy, for his great love wherewith he loved us, even when we were dead in sins, hath quickened us together with Christ (by grace ye are saved), and hath raised us up together, and made us sit together in heavenly places in Christ Jesus.'

> Let us use the argument of our own case. 1. Once we were as far from God as you. Once we, like you, cared only for fulfilling our corrupt heart's desires. We were as guilty as you, exposed to God's wrath. 2. But God, of his own good will, awoke us to feel our evil state. 3. God has brought us into a most blessed state. We feel unspeakably happy, for we have been made partners with Christ in what he did on our behalf. 4. We possess a peace and joy that you never knew. Would you not seek it in the way we obtained it?

Psa. 14:1. 'The fool hath said in his heart, There is no God.'

Jude 14-15. 'Behold, the Lord cometh with ten thousands of his saints, to execute judgment upon all, and to convince all that are ungodly among them of all their ungodly deeds which they have ungodly committed, and of all their hard speeches which ungodly sinners have spoken against him.'

> As Paul testified to Felix, so do you testify to the most sceptical. Speak solemnly of that Day. Christ will then *convince* men who doubt and deny now. He will show the wickedness of their *deeds,* and of their *speeches* too.

1 Sam. 2:2. 'There is none holy as the Lord.'

Isa. 6:3. 'Holy, holy, holy, is the Lord of Hosts.'

Job 9:4. 'He is wise in heart, and mighty in strength. Who hath hardened himself against him and hath prospered? Which removeth the mountains, and they know not, which overturneth them in his anger, which shaketh the earth out of her place.'

Job 9:11-12. 'Lo, he goeth by me and I see him not: he passeth on also and I perceive him not. Behold, he taketh away, who can hinder him? Who will say unto him, What doest thou!'

Obad. 3-4. 'The pride of thine heart hath deceived thee, thou that dwellest in the clefts of the rocks, whose habitation is high; that saith in his heart, Who shall bring me down to the ground? Though thou exalt thyself as the eagle, and though thou set thy nest among the stars, thence will I bring thee down, saith the Lord."

Prov. 1:22-23. 'How long, ye simple ones, will ye love simplicity, and the scorners delight in their scorning, and fools hate knowledge? Turn ye at my reproof. Behold, I will pour out my Spirit unto you, I will make known my words unto you.'

> Laying aside scorning, listen to his glad tidings. He will tell you words that reveal the very heart of God. He will give his own Spirit too.

Ezek. 18:25. 'Yet ye say, The way of the Lord is not

equal. Hear now, O house of Israel, is not my way equal? are not your ways unequal?' So verse 25. But verse 30. 'Therefore I will judge you, O house of Israel, everyone according to his ways.'

Ezek. 18:30. 'Repent, and turn yourselves from all your transgressions, so iniquity shall not be your ruin. Cast away from you all your transgressions whereby ye have transgressed, and make ye a new heart and a new spirit. For why will ye die, O house of Israel?'

> Here God uses authority, and yet compassion and tender mercy too. It is for our own interest's sake that he thus condescends to reason with us.

Psa. 146:4. 'His breath goeth forth, he returneth to his earth; in that very day, his thoughts perish.'

> '*His thoughts perish*'—all his theories—all his opinions—all his philosophy. The stern reality of the judgment seat and of the holy Judge dissipates all vain hopes and fancies.

Rom. 6:23. 'The wages of sin is death.'

Isa. 57:10. 'Thou art wearied in the greatness of thy way.'

> 1. Is it not true that up to this moment the issue of all thy many attempts to find satisfaction has been disappointment?
> 2. Listen, then, to one who is sent to such as thou. Isa. 1:4.

Psa. 49:6-9. 'They that trust in their wealth, and boast themselves in the multitude of their riches; none of them can by any means redeem his brother, nor give to God a ransom for him; for the redemption of their soul is precious, and it ceaseth for ever [the attempt to give the price is a continual failure], that he should live for ever, and not see corruption.'

> O solemn, solemn certainty. 1. None can save a brother from the grave. 2. None can save a soul. 3. You can offer no ransom money.

Mark 8:36-37. 'For what shall it profit a man, if he shall gain the whole world and lose his own soul? Or what shall a man give in exchange for his soul?'

> 1. Think what a lost soul loses! It loses earth, heaven, God. It loses in the same moment all hope. 2. What is the world worth in such an hour? 3. If once lost, what *'exchange'*, *i.e.* what ransom to set you free from that prison-house could you ever find? And yet what would you not then give if you could?

Ezek. 33:11. 'Say unto them, As I live, saith the Lord God, I have no pleasure in the death of the wicked, but that the wicked turn from his way and live. Turn ye, turn ye, from your evil ways; for why will ye die?'

Luke 19:41-42. 'He beheld the city and wept over it, saying, If thou hadst known, even thou, at least in this thy day, the things which belong unto thy peace.'

> See the sincere tears of Christ—wept over the most hardened. Thereby be persuaded of these three things: 1. There

is tremendous woe, a hell for ever, awaiting the lost. 2. God feels deep pity even for the lost. 3. It is, therefore, nothing but sin that renders it necessary that these souls should perish. Sin is the poison that destroys them for ever.

John 5:39-40. '[The Scriptures] testify of me; and ye will not come to me, that ye may have life.'

Jer. 13:16-17. 'Give glory to the Lord your God before he cause darkness, and your feet stumble upon the dark mountains, and while ye look for light, he turn it into the shadow of death, and make it gross darkness. But if ye will not hear it, my soul shall weep in secret places for your pride, and mine eye shall weep sore.'

Rom. 5:20. 'Where sin abounded, grace did much more abound.'

Psa. 68:18. 'Thou hast received gifts for men; yea, for the rebellious also, that the Lord God may dwell among them.'

2 Kings 1:2-4. 'And Ahaziah sent messengers and said unto them, Go, inquire of Baal-zebub, the god of Ekron, whether I shall recover of this disease. But the angel of the Lord said unto Elijah the Tishbite, Arise, go up to meet the messengers of the king of Samaria, and say unto them, Is it not because there is not a God in Israel, that ye go to inquire of Baal-zebub, the god of Ekron? Now, therefore, thus saith the Lord, Thou shalt not come down from the bed on which thou art gone up, but shalt surely die.'

Psa. 107:10-13. 'Such as sit in darkness, and in the shadow of death, being bound in affliction and iron; because they rebelled against the words of God, and contemned the counsel of the Most High. Therefore he brought down their heart with labour; they fell, and there was none to help. Then they cried unto the Lord in their trouble, and he saved them out of their distresses.

Isa. 33:14. 'The sinners in Zion are afraid; fearfulness hath surprised the hypocrites. Who among us shall dwell with the devouring fire? Who among us shall dwell with everlasting burnings?'

Heb. 10:27. 'A fearful looking for of judgment.'

Matt. 8:29. 'And behold they cried out, saying, What have we to do with thee, Jesus, thou Son of God? Art thou come hither to torment us before the time?'

> The cry of *devils*. But *men* cannot say this, for Prov. 8:4, brings us the Lord's message thus: 'Unto you, O men, do I call, and my voice is to the sons of men.'

Matt. 26:64. 'Nevertheless I say unto you, hereafter ye shall see the Son of man sitting on the right hand of power, and coming in the clouds of heaven.'

> 1. Whatever be your present scepticism, 'Nevertheless hereafter ye shall see.' 2. It was thus Christ himself dealt with a scoffer and an infidel.

Introduction to Chapter 10

The Sick Person Is Indifferent

I. As the visitor sets out, let him think of the Holy Spirit, Zech. 12:10, how he can cause mourning for sin — deep, heartfelt, soul-piercing mourning — and how he can lift the eye to the Saviour.

2. Pray, also, for *'long-suffering'* to yourself, like our Lord's when he said, Luke 13:34, 'O Jerusalem, Jerusalem, how often would I have gathered thy children . . . and ye would not.' We are ready, in a case like this, to grow weary, to speak languidly, to be hopeless, and, perhaps, to give up altogether.

3. Try *rousing* words. Such are Eph. 2:12. Tell what that implies — no Christ, no God, no hope. Or Mark 16:16, tell what 'damnation' means, and how it comes. Show the sick one that it is the sinner himself that puts the torch to the pile of Tophet.

Try *drawing* words. Such are Isaiah 1:18, 'Come now, let us reason together, *saith the Lord'*; &c. It is *God* (not you) that stands at that bedside and kindly invites. His offer is the very greatest ever made, altogether affecting our interests—the offer of salvation, if we hear his voice.

Try a *question* like Jer. 13:21, 'What wilt thou say when he shall punish thee?' or, Mal. 3:2, 'But who may abide the day of his coming?'

Persevere in declaring the *good news* of God's grace to the guilty. But we must never be formal in so doing. We must every time tell what we have felt and have been using for ourselves.

10

THE SICK PERSON IS INDIFFERENT

Eph. 2:12. 'Without Christ—having no hope—without God in the world.'

Hos. 7:2. 'They consider not in their hearts that I remember all their wickedness.'

Jer. 5:3, 6. 'Thou hast stricken them, and they have not grieved; thou hast consumed them, but they have refused to receive correction: they have made their faces harder than a rock; they have refused to return . . . Therefore, a lion out of the forest shall slay them [*i.e.* some strong unsparing foe]; and a wolf of the evenings shall spoil them [*i.e.* some greedy foe]; a leopard shall watch over their cities [some cunning foe].'

Isa. 26:11. 'Lord, when thy hand is lifted up they will not see. But they shall see and be ashamed.'[1]

---

[1] 'This blindness is like the tying of the handkerchief over the face of the criminal, in order to his being turned off into hell.'—*Flavel.*

John 3:18. 'Condemned already'.

Mark 16:16. 'Damned'.

Psa. 73:4-5. 'For there are no bands in their death; but their strength is firm. They are not in trouble as other men, neither are they plagued as other men.'

> This is the most alarming feature of their condition. No fear, no faith, no feeling. But what is the end? O that they would but give ear, verse 19.

Num. 32:23. 'Behold ye have sinned against the Lord, and be sure your sin will find you out.'

Hos. 10:12. 'Sow to yourselves in righteousness; reap in mercy; break up your fallow ground; for it is time to seek the Lord, till he come and rain righteousness upon us.'

Eccles. 3:15. 'God requireth that which is past.'

Eccles. 12:14. 'For God shall bring every work into judgment, with every secret thing, whether it be good, or whether it be evil.'

Mark 9:43-44. 'Into hell, into the fire that never shall be quenched; where their worm [each one's special worm] dieth not, and the fire is not quenched.' Verses 45-46. 'Into hell, into the fire that never shall be quenched; where their worm dieth not, and the fire is not quenched.' Verses 47-48. 'Into hell-fire, where their worm dieth not, and the fire is not quenched.'

Psa. 73:19. 'How are they brought into desolation, as in a moment! They are utterly consumed with terrors. As a dream when one awaketh . . .'

Mic. 6:9. 'The Lord's voice crieth . . . Hear ye the rod.'

Amos 4:11. 'Prepare to meet thy God.'

Ezek. 22:14. 'Can thine heart endure, or can thine hands be strong, in the days that I shall deal with thee?'[2]

Heb. 11:7. 'By faith Noah, being warned of God of things not seen as yet, moved with fear, prepared an ark to the saving of his house.'

> 1. You, too, are warned of a coming flood—of the 'wrath to come'. 2. You, too, are warned that God's 'Spirit will not always strive with man'. 3. There is an ark, Christ Jesus, built without your aid, ready open. 4. Let fear of wrath turn your eye to that Ark; for when it is shut, men will cry in agony, 'The great day of his wrath is come, and who shall be able to stand?'

Psa. 50:21-22. 'These things thou hast done, and I kept silence; thou thoughtest that I was altogether such an one as thyself. But I will reprove thee and set them in order before thine eyes. Now, consider this, ye that forget God; lest I tear you in pieces, and there be none to deliver.'

Psa. 90:11. 'Who knoweth the power of thine anger?'

Matt. 24:38-39. 'For as it was in the days that were before the flood, . . . they knew not until the flood came and took them all away. So shall also the coming of the Son of man be.'

---

[2] 'I marvel', says one, 'at the stupidity of men: but most of all at my own stupidity.'

Jer. 2:12-13. 'Be astonished, O ye heavens, at this, and be horribly afraid; be ye very desolate, saith the Lord. For my people have committed two evils, they have forsaken me the fountain of living waters, and hewed them out cisterns, broken cisterns, that can hold no water.'

> How awful this repetition of such solemn, tremendous truths!

Luke 16:23-24. 'In hell he lifted up his eyes, being in torments, and seeth Abraham afar off, and Lazarus in his bosom . . . Send Lazarus, that he may dip the tip of his finger in water and cool my tongue; for I am tormented in this flame.'

Luke 16:26. 'And besides all this, between us and you there is a great gulf fixed; so that they which would pass hence to you cannot; neither can they pass to us that would come from thence.'

Lev. 6:13. 'The fire shall ever be burning on the altar. It shall never go out.'

> 1. The justice of God never, never changes, nor foregoes its demand. 2. Hell will show this. 3. The cross shows it.

Zeph. 1:7-8. 'Hold thy peace at the presence of the Lord God; for the day of the Lord is at hand; for the Lord hath prepared a sacrifice; he hath bid his guests. And it shall come to pass, in the day of the Lord's sacrifice, that I will punish the princes and the king's children, and all such as are clothed in strange apparel.'

1. A *sacrifice* is mentioned here, but it is not like that on the altar; it is OF men, not FOR men. 2. They that will not come to the *atoning sacrifice,* shall find themselves guests at this sacrifice of slaughter—*their own lives poured* out in God's fierce anger.

Jer. 13:21. 'What wilt thou say when he shall punish thee?'[3]

Acts 17:30-31. 'The times of this ignorance God winked at; but now commandeth all men, everywhere, to repent: because, he hath appointed a day in which he will judge the world in righteousness by that man whom he hath ordained.'

1. Once, God seemed as if he saw not; he let you go on in your ways. 2. Now, God has taken notice of you and your sins, and commands you to repent. 3. He has lifted up Christ, as the brazen serpent was lifted up, to the view of all men, even unto the ends of the earth, saying, 'Look and be saved'; and therefore he calls on all men without exception, in all places without exception, and therefore on *you.* 4. He urges you to this because yonder is the day of wrath—Christ is coming to take vengeance on all that know not God, and obey not the gospel.

Jer. 5:22. 'Fear ye not me, saith the Lord? Will ye not tremble at my presence which have placed the sand for the bound of the sea by a perpetual decree that it cannot pass it; and though the waters thereof toss themselves,

---

[3] 'The good man's best, and the bad man's worst, are to come, Isa. 3:9. Men that like sin's work, will not like sin's wages.'—*R. Venning.*

yet can they not prevail; though they roar, yet can they not pass over it?'

> If he is a God who can bind in the sea by such a simple and apparently feeble band as the sea-sand, think of what he can do to sinners. In spite of all their tossing and raging, his perpetual decree will hold them fast.

Isa. 28:17-18. 'Judgment will I lay to the line, and righteousness to the plummet; and the hail shall sweep away the refuge of lies, and the waters shall overflow the hiding-place; and your covenant with death shall be disannulled, and your agreement with hell shall not stand.'

> You seem *as if* you had got *death* and *hell* to agree not to harm you. But on what does this persuasion rest? What if your hiding-place be a 'refuge of lies'? 1. Is it this: There is no great harm in sin? 2. Or, I am not so bad as many. 3. Or, God is merciful. 4. Or, I hope to be converted yet, at a more convenient season. 5. Or, There will be few lost. 6. Or, I am doing all I can. 7. Or, There is a change begun in me; old things are passed away. 8. Or, I am resigned to God's will. 9. Or, Whom else but Christ could I rest on! 10. Or, I hope I am converted already, for I have had great convictions. 11. Or, I think I once believed. 12. Or, I have many of the marks of a believer. Some of these may be your 'refuge of lies'. Or possibly it may be *duties, sorrow for sin, imitation of God's people,* and the like.
>
> There is no 'hiding-place' but one, *viz., Christ him-self*—not what you do and feel, but what Christ has done: and this you must make use of.

Isa. 33:14. 'Who among us shall dwell with the devouring fire? Who among us shall dwell with everlasting burnings?'

Gal. 6:7. 'Be not deceived, God is not mocked; for whatsoever a man soweth that shall he also reap.'

Mal. 3:2. 'But who may abide the day of his coming?'

Isa. 10:3. 'And what will ye do in the day of visitation, and in the desolation that shall come from far? To whom will ye flee for help? And where will ye leave your glory?'

Acts 4:12 (last clause). *'We must be saved!'* The whole runs thus: 'Neither is there salvation in any other; for there is none other name given under heaven, among men, whereby we must be saved.'

Isa. 1:18. 'Come, now [*i.e. Come, I pray thee*], let us reason together, saith the Lord; though your sins be as scarlet, they shall be as white as snow; though they be red like crimson, they shall be as wool.'

> Not 'Come, and I will show you what to do', but 'Come and let me tell you *what I have done,* by which scarlet and crimson sins become white.'

Isa. 1:20. 'But if ye refuse and rebel, ye shall be devoured with the sword; for the mouth of the Lord has spoken it.'[4]

---

[4] 'God's sword has two edges. It can cut back-stroke and fore-stroke. If his word do thee no good, it will do thee hurt. It is the saviour of life to those that receive it, but of death to those that refuse it.'—*Bunyan.*

Isa. 27:4-5. 'I would go through them, I would burn them together; or, let him take hold of my strength, that he may make peace with me; and he shall make peace with me.'

> 1. This is the only place where *man* is said to *make* peace with God. It evidently means, 'Let him *enter into peace* with me'; it does not mean that man furnishes the grounds of peace, or gives God anything in order to induce him to be at peace. 2. God's strong arm holds out the peace, ready made; let the sinner take it.

Eph. 2:14. 'He is our peace.' Connect this with verse 13. 'In Christ Jesus, ye who sometimes were afar off are made nigh by the blood of Christ.'

Col. 1:20. 'Having made peace through the blood of his cross.'

1 John 5:11-12. 'This is the record, that God hath given to us eternal life, and this life is in his Son. He that hath the Son hath life.'

1 John 5:10, 12. 'He that believeth not God, hath made him a liar . . . He that hath not the Son of God, hath not life.'

Mark 16:16. 'He that believeth shall be saved.'

PART II

THE WORD BROUGHT NEAR TO SEVEN CLASSES WHO MAY BE FOUND IN THE SICK ROOM

INTRODUCTION TO CHAPTER 11

RECOVERY FROM SICKNESS—
THE BELIEVER'S CASE

I. In 2 Tim. 1:14, we read, 'That good thing . . . *keep by the Holy Ghost which dwelleth in thee.*' A believer recovering from sickness feels that he needs the Holy Ghost to do what David prayed for in 1 Chron. 29:18. 'O Lord God of Abraham, Isaac, and Israel, keep this for ever in the imagination of the thoughts of the heart of thy people, and prepare their heart unto thee.' On this account, *prayer* with such is most suitable.

2. *Praise* should be stirred up. Take perhaps Psa. 107:20-21. Here is one receiving God's mercies, and affected thereby; 'He sent his word and healed them. Oh that men would praise the Lord for his goodness!'

3. It is suitable to recall sins to mind. For 'the best way to be made to praise for our mercies is to be affected with our sins.'—*Hill.*

4. Sometimes take such a passage as John 9:4, and urge it: 'I must work the works of him that sent me, while it is day. The night cometh, when no man can work.' After a time of trouble, wherein the shades of night seemed to be settling down, how seasonable is the call to work, and work much, and work well, and work now.

11

RECOVERY FROM SICKNESS—
THE BELIEVER'S CASE

Psa. 107:20-22. 'He sent his word and healed them, and delivered them from their destructions. Oh that men would praise the Lord for his goodness, and for his wonderful works to the children of men: and let them sacrifice the sacrifices of thanksgiving, and declare his works with rejoicing.'

Psa. 107:2-4. 'Bless the Lord, O my soul, and forget not all his benefits; who forgiveth all thine iniquities, who healeth all thy diseases; who redeemeth thy life from destruction; who crowneth thee with loving-kindness and tender mercies.'

Judg. 5:11. 'They that are delivered from the noise of archers, in the places of drawing water, there they shall rehearse the righteous acts of the Lord, even the righteous acts towards the inhabitants of his villages.'

> N.B. — *'There* they shall' — on the spot where the deliverance is received, and at the time when all is fresh in their mind.

Heb. 12:9. 'We have had fathers of our flesh which corrected us, and we gave them reverence; shall we not much rather be in subjection unto the Father of our spirits, and live?'

> In the former case, all we did was to be silent, and submit from a sense of filial duty. But in the latter, shall we not at the same time look for a life-giving result attending on the discipline?

Heb. 12:11. 'Now no chastening for the present seemeth to be joyous, but grievous. Nevertheless afterward it yieldeth the peaceable fruits of righteousness unto them which are exercised thereby.'

> See, it is *'afterward'* that the fruit is to be reaped. For, like ground lying fallow, body and soul seem ofttimes left useless and neglected in sickness; or, we may say, like winter wheat, the seed lies underground till the snow and frost of your sickness pass over, and then it springs up. This is the privilege of *all God's children:* for their affliction was not sent in anger, but as a means of blessing. To them *grief* is the seed of joy. So Psa. 97:11. (See again, Part III 1.)

1 Pet. 2:5, 9. 'Ye are . . . a holy priesthood, to offer up spiritual sacrifices, acceptable to God by Jesus Christ . . . A royal priesthood, a peculiar people, that ye should shew forth the praises of him who hath called you out of darkness into his marvellous light.'

> 1. Your bodily deliverance may remind you of your soul's time of distress and deliverance, and so anew call forth praise for both temporal and spiritual health. 2. The *sacrifice* is that of thanks and self-dedication and service. 3. Who else will praise and thank God, if you do not? You are the Lord's band of Levitical singers.

Psa. 51:17. 'The sacrifices of God are a broken spirit; a broken and a contrite heart, O Lord, thou wilt not despise.'

> 1. This speaks of what is the best *thank-offering*. It is the *continual offering of a heart sensible of God's grace.* 2. The woman to whom so many sins were forgiven, and who loved much, washing Christ's feet with tears and anointing them, had a 'broken and contrite heart'. She was softened and humbled, yet calmly joyful, under a mingled sense of sin and pardon of sin! 3. *This* would be your best sacrifice of thanks.

Isa. 38:9, 15. 'The writing of Hezekiah when he had been sick, and was recovered of his sickness . . . I shall go softly all my years[1] in the bitterness of my soul.'

> 1. This is, *q.d.* the bitterness of soul which I felt shall be the carpet on which I tread, the pathway by which I journey. 2. Such things are to be remembered during the whole of my afterlife, 'all my years'. 3. Keeping these in remembrance,

---

[1] 'I should wish that each cross were looked in the face seven times, and were read over and over again.'—*S. Rutherford.*

I will walk softly; feeling what I owe to God, I will live like one who treads cautiously and anxiously.

Isa. 38:16. 'O Lord, by these things men live; and in all these things is the life of my spirit; so wilt thou recover me, and make me to live.'

> 1. These distresses of body are life to the soul, and by such sore experiences men might be spiritually quickened.
> 2. This was thy purpose in the affliction; and this being accomplished, thou wilt make me to live.

Song of Sol. 8:5. 'Who is this that cometh up from the wilderness, leaning on her Beloved?'

Isa. 38:18. 'The grave cannot praise thee; death cannot celebrate thee; they that go down to the pit cannot hope for thy truth.'

> Our time of serving thee is finished with our life, *i.e.* our opportunity of serving thee among men, who might learn from us to serve our God. We cannot make thy praise heard in the grave, as Paul and Silas did in the prison; nor can we then show men how, amidst darkness, saints honour thee by expecting the fulfilment of thy word. So Psa. 6:5, and 30:9, and 115:17.

Isa. 38:19. 'The living, the living, they shall praise thee, as I do this day.'

John 9:4. 'I must work the works of him that sent me, while it is day. The night cometh when no man can work.'[2]

---

[2] 'I shall not be able to forgive myself', said one in reviewing his life, 'for

The Believer's Case

Matt. 24:43. 'But this know, that if the goodman of the house had known in what watch the thief would come, he would have watched, and would not have suffered his house to be broken up.'

> Spoken in reference to future regrets of men, when they shall lament that they did not prepare for the Lord's coming when they had time. Now, 1. Apply this to the Lord calling you away. 2. Use your present time of recovery in such a way that no such regret shall ever fill your mind. 3. *Watching* implies your being in such a position or state of soul, that in any event you are ready, and would be found prepared to meet him.

Job 36:8-12. 'And if they be bound in fetters, and holden in cords of affliction, then he sheweth them their work and their transgressions, that they have exceeded; he openeth also their ear to discipline, and commandeth that they return from iniquity. If they obey and serve him, they shall spend their days in prosperity, and their years in pleasure. But if they obey not, they shall perish by the sword, and shall die without knowledge.'

Luke 8:39. 'Return to thine own house, and shew how great things God hath done unto thee.' Mark 5:19, adds, 'And hath had compassion on thee.'

Phil. 2:27. 'God had mercy on him, and not on him only, but on me also, lest I should have sorrow upon sorrow.'

> '*Mercy*' to the restored one; for you have longer time to

---

not having served God better.'

135

labour for God. 'To me to live is Christ.' 'If I live in the flesh this is the fruit of my labour', *i.e.* this is equivalent to, or a pledge of, my having fruit of the more labour in which my prolonged time will enable me to engage.

Psa. 30:3-5. 'O Lord, thou hast brought up my soul from the grave; thou hast kept me alive, that I should not go down to the pit. Sing unto the Lord, O ye saints of his, and give thanks at the remembrance of his holiness [or, to the memorial of his holiness, *i.e.* to his holy name brought to remembrance]: for his anger endureth but a moment; in his favour is life. Weeping may endure for a night [may sojourn as a wayfarer], but joy cometh in the morning.'

Isa. 63:7. 'I will mention the loving-kindnesses of the Lord and the praises of the Lord, according to all that the Lord hath bestowed on us, and the great goodness to the house of Israel which he hath bestowed on them, according to his mercies, and according to the multitude of his loving-kindnesses.'

Acts 9:34. 'Eneas, Jesus Christ maketh thee whole!'

Eccles. 5:4. 'When thou vowest a vow unto God, defer not to pay it; for he hath no pleasure in fools. Pay that which thou hast vowed.'

> And in so doing remember Mal. 1:14, 'Cursed be the deceiver, which voweth and sacrificeth unto the Lord a corrupt thing.'

Hos. 14:8. 'What have I to do any more with idols?'

2 Chron. 32:25. 'But Hezekiah rendered not again according to the benefit done unto him; for his heart was lifted up. Therefore, there was wrath upon him, and upon Judah and Jerusalem.'

> Might not your unthankfulness bring damage—1. To your own soul? 2. To your family? 3. To your friends?

Rom. 12:15. 'Rejoice with them that do rejoice, and weep with them that weep.'

> 'Surely by these afflictions, the Lord will work in me more tenderness and compassion toward those that are afflicted.'—Thomas Brooks' *Mute Christian*.

Psa. 119:71. 'It is good for me that I have been afflicted, that I might learn thy statutes. And verse 59, 'I thought on my ways, and turned my feet unto thy testimonies.'

Esther 9:20-23. 'And Mordecai sent letters unto all the Jews that were in all the provinces of king Ahasuerus, both nigh and far, to establish this among them, that they should keep the fourteenth day of the month Adar, and the fifteenth day of the same, yearly, as the days wherein the Jews rested from their enemies, and the month which was turned unto them from sorrow into joy, and from mourning into a good day; that they should make them days of feasting and joy [a season of thankful joy to the Lord], and of sending portions one to another, and gifts to the poor. And the Jews undertook to do as they had begun.'

Philm. 11, 15. 'Which in time past was to thee unprofitable, but now profitable to thee and to me . . . For perhaps he therefore departed for a season; that thou shouldest receive him for ever.'

> How applicable to sanctified affliction! 1. Now will I live more profitably to myself and to my friends. 2. Surely this was God's design in withdrawing me for a time from my work and from my friends.

Luke 17:15-16, 19. 'And one of them, when he saw that he was healed, turned back, and with a loud voice glorified God, and fell down on his face at his feet, giving him thanks . . . And he said unto him, Arise, go thy way; thy faith hath made thee whole.'

> Has there been, in your case, any such direct and solemn acknowledgment of the Lord's kindness to you? Gladness is not gratitude. Have you felt that your recovery was undeserved mercy? and have you owned the God of grace in it all?

INTRODUCTION TO CHAPTER 12

RECOVERY FROM SICKNESS—
THE CASE OF THE NOMINAL CHRISTIAN
AND THE UNBELIEVER

IF we all need 'the Spirit which is of God, that we may know the things that are freely given to us of God' (*1 Cor.* 2:12), then surely we cannot fail to go forth to the merely nominal Christian, and the unbeliever, with the prayer: 'Spirit of God, who alone canst make known to any soul the salvation of God in its freeness and fulness, O come thou to those whom I now go to visit.'

Affliction will not of itself reveal anything of these truths to the soul. It is not a fire to melt the wax, unless the Holy Spirit be there. Without this, it may be a fire to dry the bricks.

1. Use the Word. 'A word spoken in due season, how good is it!' A word after recovery may tingle in the per-

son's ears, as no doubt did our Lord's memorable words to his healed one, 'Sin no more, lest a worse thing come unto thee' (*John* 5:14).

2. We may reason a little in the style of Ezra 9:13-14, 'And after all that is come upon us . . . should we again break thy commandments? Wouldest not thou be angry with us till thou hadst consumed us?' Ask the person—Do you feel it likely you will forget all God has been doing to you? Ask again—If you do forget, will you wonder if he *harden* you?

3. And let us always take this occasion, when the recovered man's heart is glad, to declare the gospel of God. That God who has brought him so low, and raised him up, has been giving him an emblem of how he raises from the dunghill and death of sin, and lifts up to the happy health of pardon, sending the restored and forgiven one to breathe the fresh air of divine love and the Spirit's sovereign working. Remind and impress on the recovered one that he is expected to use this respite for the end of *giving heed to the great report* (*Isa.* 53:1), and living the life of faith, waiting for God's Son from heaven.

4. Speak thus in calm faith; and return to thy house to pray.

12

Recovery from Sickness —
the Case of the Nominal Christian
and the Unbeliever

Ezra 9:13-14. 'And after all that is come upon us for our evil deeds, and for our great trespass, seeing that thou our God hast punished us less than our iniquities deserve, and hast given us such deliverance as this; should we again break thy commandments, and join in affinity with the people of these abominations? Wouldest not thou be angry with us till thou hadst consumed us, so that there shall be no remnant nor escaping?'

John 5:14. 'Jesus findeth him in the temple, and said unto him, Behold thou art made whole! Sin no more, lest a worse thing come unto thee.'

Deut. 5:29. 'Oh that there were such an heart in them, that they would fear me, and keep all my commandments always, that it might be well with them, and with their children for ever.'

> 1. See God's intense desire for your salvation. 2. Think of his eye upon you, looking for some decided result of his providential dealings with you.

Psa. 106:12-13. 'Then believed they his words; they sang his praise. They soon forgat his works; they waited not for counsel.'

Psa. 78:34-36. 'When he slew them, then they sought him; and they returned and inquired early after God; and they remembered that God was their Rock, and the High God their Redeemer. Nevertheless they did flatter him with their mouth.'

2 Pet. 2:22. 'But it happened unto them according to the true proverb, The dog is turned to his vomit again; and the sow that was washed, to her wallowing in the mire.'

Matt. 12:43-45. 'When the unclean spirit is gone out of a man, he walketh through dry places, seeking rest, and findeth none. Then he saith, I will return into my house from whence I came out; and when he is come, he findeth it empty, swept, and garnished. Then goeth he, and taketh with himself seven other spirits more wicked than himself, and they enter in and dwell there: and the last state of that man is worse than the first.

> Take heed lest this apply to thee. 1. Sickness made some change on thee; some of thy former ways were abandoned. Many things were amended, the house was garnished. But,

2. The house was left *'empty'*. The world was thrust out for a time, but Christ was not brought in to fill thy soul. 3. If *fear* made a temporary change, whilst you had no *faith* laying hold on God through Christ as thy portion, then, do not wonder if all your impressions vanish, and your reformation disappear. 3. Nay, take heed lest you become far worse, and far more hardened than ever you were before. For, 4. Christ here tells some solemn facts about the way in which devils watch such souls as yours, in cases where there seemed a temporary amendment.

2 Chron. 25:16. 'I know that God hath determined to destroy thee, because thou hast done this, and hast not hearkened unto my counsel.'

Exod. 9:27-28, 33, 35. 'I have sinned this time: the Lord is righteous, and I and my people are wicked. Entreat the Lord (for it is enough) that there be no more thunderings and hail, and I will let you go, and you shall stay no longer. . . . And Moses spread abroad his hands unto the Lord, and the thunders and hail ceased. And the heart of Pharaoh was hardened.'

1. Remember how God's servants prayed for you in your sickness, and remember your anxiety to be delivered. Remember your resolutions and acknowledgments. Remember how serious everything then seemed. 2. Remember God's great grace—how he heard, pitied, delivered, showed kindness to you; and how he asks only this of you, that you would now slake your thirst in the river of life, and live in the enjoyment of his love. 3. Would you be as Pharaoh?

Ezek. 24:13-14. 'Because I have purged thee, and thou wast not purged, thou shalt not be purged from thy filthiness any more, till I have caused my fury to rest upon thee. I the Lord have spoken it; it shall come to pass, and I will do it; I will not go back, neither will I spare, neither will I repent.'

Luke 13:8-9. 'Lord, let alone this year also, till I shall dig about it, and dung it. And if it bear fruit, well. And if not, then, after that, thou shalt cut it down.'

> The spared fig-tree is expected to bear fruit. Here is—
> 1. Christ's long-suffering grace, interceding when the axe is lifted up. 2. A time fixed, however, for even such grace ending. 3. Does thy soul not feel moved and melted?

Gen. 6:3. 'My Spirit shall not always strive with man; for that he also is flesh.'

Amos 4:11-12. 'I have overthrown some of you, as God overthrew Sodom and Gomorrha, and ye were as a fire-brand plucked out of the burning. Yet ye have not returned unto me, saith the Lord. Therefore, thus will I do unto thee, O Israel.'

Zeph. 3:2. 'She obeyed not the voice;' [this was God's proclamation of his will in ordinances and public messages.] 'She received not correction'; [this was God's dealing by afflictive providences]. 'She trusted not in the Lord; she drew not near to her God.' The result is, 'Woe to her that is filthy', verse 1.

Zeph. 3:7. 'I said, Surely, thou wilt fear me; thou wilt receive instruction, so thy dwelling should not be cut off, howsoever I punished them: but they rose early, and corrupted all their doings.'[1]

1 Sam. 24:18-19. 'Thou hast shewed this day, how that thou hast dealt well with me; forasmuch as when the Lord had delivered me into thine hand, thou killedst me not. For, if a man find his enemy, will he let him go well away?' And verse 16, At the time he spoke these words, 'Saul lifted up his voice and wept.'

> If such a one as Saul was so deeply moved by the sparing kindness of David, what may be expected of you? 1. You have been God's foe. 2. In your sickness you were sleeping with the sword of wrath over your head. 3. Nay, more, that sickness which well-nigh cut you off was to show you how God might in a moment have ended your days; it was the cutting off the skirt of your robe; ay, and this day, your pale face and weakened frame are like God's voice, saying, 'See, the skirt of your robe is in my hand. I cut off the skirt of your robe, yet killed you not.' 4. What shall the end be? Is this your voice, O God, to me, and shall I not evermore give glory to your name?

Luke 17:17-18. 'And Jesus answering, said, Were there not ten cleansed? but where are the nine? There are not found that returned to give glory to God save this stranger.'

---

[1] 'The rod is an evil in itself, and will do us no good but evil, unless the Lord make it a blessing to us.' — *Caryl.*

1. Christ delights to see healed men thankful. 2. Christ grieves over the unthankful.

2 **Chron.** 27:22. 'And in the time of his distress did he trespass yet more against the Lord. This is that king Ahaz.'

Introduction to Chapter 13

For the Aged Who Are Sick

There is often a natural torpor, or something of the kind, in the faculties of the old whom we may be called to visit. But let us remember that the Holy Ghost can remove this hindrance; let us be encouraged by the thought of his kindness to old Simeon; 'The Holy Ghost was upon him' (*Luke* 2:25-26), and in his old age, he saw salvation and the Saviour in a way he had never seen before.

1. It is sometimes useful to remind the old of the past, even as far back as infancy and childhood. That view of sin, and of corruption as it then manifested itself, is fitted to leave deep sense of need on their souls. A long life of sin; so many sins during threescore years; so great sins among these many! all these many and great sins recorded by God, and to be spoken of to me soon, very soon, at the judgment-seat!

Remember that as things done some time before, or in youth, are generally the things best remembered by the old, so it is in this way we may most readily get them to dwell upon their sins. Try, then, such a text as Jer. 31:19.

2. Show the depth and power of the fountain that can cleanse such; and show the grace that calls on them to come, though now their joints be trembling, their eyes dazzled, their heart fainting, their limbs failing, their body full of aches and diseases, their heart ready to sink.

3. A question, such as, *'Are you born again?'* or, *'Were you ever converted?'* or, *'Is there any period in all your past life to which you can point as a time when God revealed his Son in you?'* has been found useful in startling dormant minds into thoughtfulness.

4. If it be an old Simeon you visit, speak little else but the words of God. Visit with him favourite places of the Word. Stir him up to praise.

5. In the case of such a Simeon, press on him the opportunity still left him of helping the church of God, by being like Moses on the hill, who failed not to pray while Joshua fought with Amalek.

6. Remind him of Heb. 3:14, ' We are made [or, *have been made*] partakers of Christ, if we hold the beginning of our confidence stedfast to the end.' We need no other salvation than that which we began with; no other ground of confidence than that furnished by the finished work of Christ. And our going on to the end without adding to, and without being moved from this one sufficient ground, is a proof and token of the soundness of the work of grace in our hearts.

13

FOR THE AGED WHO ARE SICK

Eccles. 1:14-15. 'I have seen all the works that are done under the sun, and behold all is vanity and vexation of spirit. That which is crooked cannot be made straight, and that which is wanting cannot be numbered.'

1. A long life tests earth, and proves it a broken cistern. 2. No human skill can remedy evils, making the crooked straight, or inserting the lacking cipher. 3. Shall not this turn the eye to him of whom Solomon's father sings, Psa. 39:7, 'And now, Lord, what wait I for? my hope is in thee.'[1]

Jer. 31:19. 'I was ashamed, yea, even confounded, because I did bear the reproach of my youth.'

1 Pet. 3:20. 'Once the long-suffering of God waited in the days of Noah, while the ark was a preparing.'

Apply this to the old man's case; God waiting during his

---

[1] 'God dries up the channels, that you may be compelled to plunge into an infinite ocean of happiness.'—*R. Hall.*

long life, with the ark in sight. But the ark is soon to be shut now. If the door of the ark be shut, then the gate of hell opens.

Deut. 8:15-16. 'Who led thee through that great and terrible wilderness, wherein were fiery serpents, and scorpions, and drought; who brought thee forth water out of the rock of flint; who fed thee in the wilderness with manna, which the fathers knew not, that he might humble thee, and that he might prove thee, to do thee good at thy latter end?'

> 1. Review God's ways to you during your life. 2. See the tendency of all his dealings.

Deut. 4:9-10. 'Only take heed to thyself, and keep thy soul diligently, lest thou forget the things which thine eyes have seen, and lest they depart from thy heart, all the days of thy life; but teach them thy sons, and thy sons' sons. Specially the day that thou stoodest before the Lord thy God in Horeb.'

> 1. Have you pondered the Lord's ways toward you during life? 2. Have you nothing to tell your children and grandchildren? 3. Have you nothing to tell them of a day of awakening? a day of meeting with God? a day at Horeb?

Neh. 9:30-31. 'Many years didst thou forbear them, and testifiedst against them, by the Spirit in thy prophets; yet would they not give ear. Nevertheless, for thy great mercies' sake, thou didst not utterly consume them, nor forsake them; for thou art a gracious and merciful God.'

> Has not thy lifetime proved God to be gracious? Think of thy many years' resistance to his Spirit, who was striving with thy conscience in ordinances and providences. And yet he waits still.

1 Chron. 29:15-16. 'We are strangers before thee, and sojourners, as were all our fathers; our days on earth are as a shadow, and there is none abiding. O Lord our God, all this store that we have prepared to build thee an house for thine holy name, cometh of thine hand, and is all thine own.'

> Here is David in old age, near death. 1. He feels life a shadow departing. 2. He has used his means and his time well, and has the satisfaction of seeing that he is leaving things in train for advancing the cause of God. 3. His chief joy is in owning and adoring God, whom he has so often sung to on his harp.

Gen. 47:9. 'The days of the years of my pilgrimage are an hundred and thirty years; few and evil have the days of the years of my life been.'

> 1. How long must *eternity* be, since so long a life seems brief in comparison! 2. How *evil* is *life*, both as to adversity and sin, if seen by an eye that can discern!

Job 20:4-5, 8, 11. 'Knowest thou not this of old, since man was placed upon the earth, that the triumphing of the wicked is short? He shall fly away as a dream, and shall not be found. His bones are full of the sin of his youth,[2] which shall lie down with him in the dust.'

> This should surely lead the old man to the Psalmist's prayer, Psa. 25:7, 'Remember not the sins of my youth.'

Psa. 89:47. 'Remember how short my time is.'

Psa. 90:15. 'Make us glad according to the days wherein thou hast afflicted us, and the years wherein we have seen evil.'

> As it was with Jacob in Goshen, and with Job, 42:12.

Psa. 71:18-19. 'Now also, when I am old and grey-headed, O God, forsake me not, until I have shewed thy strength to this generation, and thy power to everyone that is to come. Thy righteousness also, O God, is very high.'

> 1. Here is a saint seeking grace to use his last days in the way of giving a testimony to the Lord's power; telling what he knows of the Lord's acts of might to the sons of men. 2. God's righteousness is another favourite theme—God righteous in his providence, righteous in his judgments, righteous in receiving sinners through his beloved Son.

Job 5:26. 'Thou shalt come to thy grave in a full age, like as a shock of corn cometh in his season.'

> Ripened by the sun and genial breezes, the corn is at last gathered. So the believer is ripened by the Spirit glorifying Christ in his soul.

---

[2] 'I seal what I assert,—the old ashes of the sins of my youth are now fires of sorrow to me.'—*S. Rutherford.*

Psa. 111:16. 'With long life will I satisfy him, and shew him my salvation.'

> 1. The Lord will give as much of life here as the believer would desire were he to see the end from the beginning; and then, the endless life of glory, the day of days which will make all former days forgotten. 2. He will at last show *full salvation, i.e.* not only (as enjoyed here) deliverance from guilt, and partial victory over indwelling sin, but deliverance from all sorrow and all the other effects of sin; and the possession of what is meant by Paul when he said, Rom. 13:11, 'Now is our salvation nearer than when we believed'; Heb. 9:28, 'He shall appear the second time . . . unto salvation.'

Deut. 33:25. 'As thy days so shall thy strength be.'

> Thy strength lasts so long as it is required to last.

2 John 1:8. 'The elder unto the elect lady . . . Look to yourselves, that we lose not those things which we have wrought, but that we receive a full reward.'

> Here is an aged saint admonishing another to persevere to the end in lively faith, and to join with him in seeking a full reward for a lifetime's service.

3 John 2. 'Beloved, I wish above all things, that thou mayest prosper, and be in health, even as thy soul prospereth.'

> By these words, John, writing to old Gaius, intimates that that aged saint flourished in grace, like Psa. 92:14, 'They shall still bring forth fruit in old age; they shall be fat and flourishing.'

Psa. 92:14-15. 'In old age, they shall be fat and flourishing, to shew that the Lord is upright.'

> 1. It was not excitement, nor the vigour of youth, that made them zealous and holy; it was the Lord's grace; and that continues still. 2. The Lord continues to visit their souls, because he is faithful to his word, and has said, 'I will never leave thee.' And again, 'Him that cometh unto me I will in no wise *cast out*' (*John* 6:37), *q.d.* I will not do to him as was done to Ishmael—I will cherish him in his old age and infirmities.

Rev. 1:4-7. 'John to the seven churches . . . Unto him that loved us, and washed us from our sins in his own blood, and hath made us kings and priests unto God and his Father; to him be glory and dominion for ever and ever, Amen! Behold, he cometh with clouds, and every eye shall see him.'

> These are the words of aged John, now about ninety, when left alone in Patmos. His fellow apostles are all gone. He is an exile from Christian brethren. He is soon to die, being now laden with years. Yet what a song he sings! He is as if already before the throne, looking back to Christ's first coming, and forward to his second.

Dan. 12:8-9, 13. 'Then said I, O my Lord, what shall be the end of these things? And he said, Go thy way, Daniel. Go thy way till the end be; for thou shalt rest, and stand in thy lot in the end of the days.'

> An aged saint, anxious about God's cause, is comforted.

1. He is bid leave these things in God's hand. 2. He is reminded of God's having rest ready for him — 'rest from his labours'. 3. He is promised a share in the resurrection of the just, a 'lot' or portion in the kingdom.

John 21:18-22. 'Verily, verily, I say unto thee, When thou wast young, thou girdest thyself, and walkedst whither thou wouldest: but when thou shalt be old, thou shall stretch forth thy hands, and another shall gird thee, and carry thee whither thou wouldest not. This spake he, signifying by what death he should glorify God. And when he had spoken this, he saith unto him, Follow me. Then Peter, turning about, seeth the disciple whom Jesus loved, following . . . Peter, seeing him, saith, Lord, and what shall this man do? Jesus saith unto him, If I will that he tarry till I come, what is that to thee? Follow thou me!'

1. Christ speaks to Peter of his old age, when he and 'Paul the aged' (*Philm.* 9) were to suffer death at Rome for his name. 2. Peter is told of a wide contrast between the days of his youth by the Sea of Galilee, when he used to gird on his fisher's coat (*John* 21:7), and these last scenes: and yet, thus *'he glorified God'*. 3. *'Follow me',* keep me ever before thee, let me be ever in thine eye. This is enough to give light even in that dark valley. Though Peter failed in younger years, when he boasted he would go to prison and to death for Christ, yet he shall 'glorify God' now by prison and death, his faith not failing while he 'follows the Lord'. 4. He is told to leave the case of friends, and their lot, on the Master. They are the Master's burden, not his.

Psa. 119:54. 'Thy statutes have been my songs in the house of my pilgrimage.'

2 Pet. 1:13-14. 'Yea, I think it meet, as long as I am in his tabernacle, to stir you up, by putting you in remembrance; knowing that shortly I must put off this my tabernacle, even as our Lord Jesus Christ hath showed me.'

John 16:31-33. 'Do ye now believe? Behold, the hour cometh, yea is now come, that ye shall be scattered, every man to his own, and shall leave me alone; and yet I am not alone, because the Father is with me. These things have I spoken unto you, that in me ye might have peace.'

2 Tim. 4:7-8. 'I have fought a good fight, I have finished my course, I have kept the faith. Henceforth, there is laid up for me a crown of righteousness, which the Lord, the righteous Judge, shall give me at that day.'

> 1. The fight I have been engaged in has been one worth the toil and risk—'good'. 2. I have run a race, and am at the goal now. 3. All along I have kept my eye on Christ, believing what is testified of him and by him. 4. I expect, on the day of his coming, the crown of righteousness. Such is dying Paul's experience, faith, hope. How full and simple.

Joshua 23:14. 'And, behold, this day I am going the way of all the earth, and ye know in all your hearts and in all your souls, that not one thing hath failed of all the good things which the Lord your God spake.'

Gen. 49:18. 'I have waited for thy salvation, O Lord.'

Old Jacob, when 130 years, is looking for the full and complete salvation which Messiah would bring, the beginnings of which he had got. Compare Rom. 13:11; Heb. 9:28.

Gen. 48:10, 15-16. 'Now the eyes of Israel were dim for age, so that he could not see . . . The God before whom my fathers Abraham and Isaac did walk, the God who fed me all my life long unto this day, the Angel which redeemed me from all evil, bless the lads.'

> 1. An aged saint's testimony. 2. An aged saint's prayer for the young.

1 John 2:13. 'I write unto you, fathers, because ye have known him that is from the beginning.'

> You who have been long in Christ; you who may be called the familiar friends of the Eternal, the Ancient of Days. Does this describe you? Have you this fellowship? Is it characteristic of you in your old age?

Titus 2:2-3. 'Aged men, be sober, grave, temperate . . . The aged women likewise.'

> 1. Be sober, or *'watchful'*, as those who may be called away at any moment 2. Eternity is near you; let its light solemnise you. The judgment-seat is near you; let its shadow fall upon you. 3. You are soon to leave the world; sit loose to it, to its cares as well as joys. Say as Barzillai, 2 Sam. 9:34-35, 'How long have I to live that I should go up with the king unto Jerusalem? I am this day fourscore years old, and can I discern between good and evil? Can thy servant taste what I eat and drink? Can I hear any more the voice of singing-men and singing-women?'

For the Aged who are Sick

Luke 2:26, 28-29. 'And it was revealed unto him by the Holy Ghost, that he should not see death before he had seen the Lord's Christ [the *Messiah* of Jehovah] . . . Then took he him up in his arms, and blessed God, and said, Lord; now lettest thou [now thou art permitting] thy servant depart in peace.'

> 1. God's kindness to this old saint. He knew the Lord already, but the Lord wished to make him still happier and holier here before he removed him to glory — to enlarge the vessel ere he set it in the upper sanctuary. 2. Simeon had no other desire than to see Messiah come. He sat loose from all things but this one. He spoke as representative of all Old Testament saints, and of all saints ripe for glory. Hervey used these words with great delight, shortly before breathing his last.

Isa. 46:4. 'And even to your old age I am He [the same I ever was], and even to hoar hairs will I carry you. I have made and I will bear: even I will carry and will deliver you.'

> O what grace! 1. Thy long life's sins do not hinder him from presenting himself still as the God who saves to the uttermost, and who gives himself as a portion to the empty soul.[3] 2. He would fain be thy father still, and 'as a man

---

[3] 'When he says that he is God to us, he is making over to us for our enjoyment and use all his glorious attributes and excellencies; his *infinity* to be the extent of our inheritance (*Rev.* 21:7) ; his *eternity* to be the date of our happiness (*John* 14:19); his *unchangeableness* to be the rock of our rest (*Mal.* 3:6); his *wisdom* to direct us (*Psa.* 63:24); his *power* to protect us (*1 Chron.* 16:26); his *holiness* to sanctify us (*Ezek.* 16:14); his *justice* to assist us (*Rom.* 3:26); his *goodness* to reward us, in the way of grace, not of debt (*1 John* 2:25); and his *truth* to secure us the accomplishment

carrieth a sucking child, so would the Lord carry thee', in spite of thy load of guilt. 3. He that created thee is he that would redeem thee, bearing thy soul's weight. He will see to thy pardon, and also to thy complete deliverance—'I will deliver you.'

John 3:16. 'God so loved the world that he gave his only begotten Son, that whosoever believeth in him should not perish, but have eternal life.'

> *'Whosoever'*—You, aged friend, with your lifetime's sins, sins of infancy, childhood, youth, old age—you, as well as Nicodemus, the ruler, who (perhaps because he was himself old) asked, 'How can a man be born *when he is old?'* verse 4. You, whosoever you be, are called on to believe on the only-begotten Son, and have eternal life. Your eye may catch the sight of the Saviour as the last sand falls from your sand-glass. In him is life.

---

of all his promises (*Heb.* 10:23).'—*Fisher's Catechism*. See also on this topic 'The Voice of God in his Promises', by *Alleine*.

Introduction to Chapter 14

For Young Men or Women Who Are Sick

Before venturing to draw the bow, let us pray to our Father in secret. And after that, we may encourage ourselves by the thought of what the Lord spoke in regard to cases where, beforehand, we could not be sure what words were most suitable, 'It shall be given you in that same hour what ye shall speak; for it is not ye that speak, but the Spirit of your Father which speaketh in you.'—Matt. 10:20.

Sickness has arrested them, and you come to visit them in prison.

1. Be sure to speak of the sins of youth as most inexcusable. The world speaks of them as ebullitions of the warm temperament of youth, and so forth. Let us speak as do the oracles of God on this matter. To resist God with all the vigour of our body and mind! Was this not sin?

2. Speak of the special sin of unbelief in young men and maidens as *most inexcusable*. 'With one consent they began to make excuse', did not abate the wrath of the king, but inflamed it. He was wroth, *a.* at their refusing; *b.* at their ALL agreeing to refuse; *c.* at their refusing his FIRST offer.

3. Show the only gospel. For there is but one gospel. Psa. 119:9, 'Wherewithal shall a young man cleanse his way? By taking heed thereto, *according to thy word.*'

4. Remind them of *Christ,* a youth for the sake of youth, that he might, *a.* take away the sins of the young, *b.* be an example to them of holiness in fleeing youthful lusts.

All this may be useful, even if the young person is a believer. And let us never forget that the youngest '*must be born again*' by the Spirit, who was set forth under the symbol of 'water' in the Old Testament (*John* 3:3). It was a striking saying of Peden, one of the Covenanters in Scotland, that if any, young or old, were to be admitted into heaven *unrenewed,* they would cry, '*A thousand worlds to get out of heaven.*'

14

FOR YOUNG MEN OR WOMEN
WHO ARE SICK

Psa. 106:6. 'We have sinned with our fathers; we have committed iniquity; we have done wickedly.'

Psa. 119:9. 'Wherewithal shall a young man cleanse his way? By taking heed thereto according to thy word.'

> 1. There is but one rule for the young sinner and the aged, one way of cleansing. The word points you to the sacrifice for sin as the means of pardon, and to the Holy Spirit for purity. 2. You must *'take heed'* to this appointed way. This is the meaning of Psa. 50:23, 'To him that ordereth his conversation [in Hebrew, 'his way'] aright, I will shew the salvation of God.' You must order your life, your system of motives and actions 'aright', *viz.,* by God's appointed method for sinners; and then you will have reason to expect to see salvation. You must accept the provided salvation.

Titus 2:6. 'Young men likewise exhort to be sober-minded.'

1. A sick-bed is fitted to sober the soul in one way. But, 2. It is the Spirit, making use of your sickness, who must do this effectually. 3. Sober-minded views of yourself and the world differ greatly from your imagination. You are a sinner. The world passes away, and is a vain show.[1] 4. Sober-minded views of God and the life to come are such as will make you reckon all things but loss and dung in comparison with your having eternal fellowship with the Lord, and an everlasting inheritance.

Jer. 22:21-22. 'I spake unto thee in thy prosperity, but thou saidst, I will not hear. This hath been thy manner from thy youth, that thou obeyedst not my voice. The wind shall eat up thy pastors [those who supplied thee with food]. Thy lovers shall go into captivity; surely then shalt thou be ashamed and confounded for all thy wickedness.'

> Like the prodigal reduced to beggary by the famine, wilt thou now return to thy Father? Or like Manasseh (2 *Chron.* 33:10, 13), of whom we read, 'The Lord spake to him, and he would not hear'; but 'when he was in affliction he besought the Lord his God, and humbled himself greatly before the *God of his fathers,* and prayed; and he was entreated of him.'

Job 36:13-14. 'The hypocrites in heart heap up wrath; they cry not when he bindeth them [when they are in fetters like Manasseh]. They die in youth.'

[1] 'Never seek warm fire under cold ice.' 'Now when the outer walls of the clay house are falling down, and you find your time has ebbed and run out, what thoughts have ye of idol pleasures that once were sweet?'—*S. Rutherford.*

Prov. 5:11-13. 'Lest thou mourn at the last, when thy flesh and body are consumed, and say, How have I hated instruction, and my heart despised reproof: and have not obeyed the voice of my teachers, nor inclined mine ear to them that instructed m!'

Job 13:23, 26. 'How many are mine iniquities and sins! Make me to know my transgression and my sin. For thou writest bitter things against me, and makest me to possess the iniquities of my youth' [*i.e.* thou entailest them on me].

Psa. 55:19. 'Because they have no changes, therefore they fear not God.'

> Many are ruined by health and prosperity. Changes, such as sickness and adversity, have been blest to many, leading them to fear the Lord. *Moab* is spoken of thus, Jer. 48:11, 'Moab has been at ease from his youth, and he hath settled on his lees. Therefore, his taste remained in him.' On the other hand, Ruth the Moabitess, being afflicted, was led to Jehovah by her affliction.

Jer. 3:4. 'Wilt thou not from this time say unto me, My Father, thou art the guide of my youth?'

> 1. Calamity had come on Israel (verse 3), as sickness comes on young man or maiden. Until then they seemed hardened—'thou hadst a whore's forehead; thou refusedst to be ashamed.' 2. But in his grace Jehovah stepped in then, as he seems to do by thy bedside, and asked, *'From this time* wilt thou?' 3. Wilt thou recognise him as the God who guided thy fathers, and who will be thy friend and guide? 4. Wilt thou learn to cry, 'My Father'?

Psa. 49:7. 'None of them can by any means redeem his brother, nor give to God a ransom for him.'

Luke 7:14. 'And he came and touched the bier; and he said, Young man, I say unto thee, Arise.'

1. Here is Christ's interest in you and in your mother's sorrows. 2. If he could remove death, how easily he can remove sickness. 3. Is he not the same, having the 'keys of hell and of death' able to save thy soul? 4. Will he not pity and love thy soul? Will he not remember thy mother's tears? 5. It is said, verse 15, 'And he delivered him to his mother', *q.d.* Let him be still a stay and staff to her. Young man, if spared, live for God, and for thy fellow-men's best interests. Young man, do you not feel the majesty with which Christ speaks? *'I say unto thee.'*

Acts 20:9-10, 12. 'A certain young man, named Euty-chus, . . . he sunk down with sleep and fell down from the third loft, and was taken up dead. And Paul went down, and fell on him, and embracing him, said, Trouble not yourselves, for his life is in him . . . And they brought the young man alive, and were not a little comforted.'

Here again, see, — 1. The interest taken in a young man by an apostle, and by the Lord. 2. Whether he was to blame or not for his sleep which caused the accident, see how precious is his life in their eyes. And the Lord by recording his name has shown special interest in him. 3. Paul was empowered to do for this young man what Elijah in 1 Kings 17:21, and Elisha in 2 Kings 4:34, are recorded as doing in their day. May you not infer, And so will the Lord do for my soul and body all that is needful and desirable in regard to my eternal welfare?'

2 Sam. 18:33. 'And the king was much moved, and went up to the chamber over the gate, and wept; and as he went, thus he said, O my son Absalom! my son, my son Absalom! Would God I had died for thee, O Absalom, my son, my son!'

> 1. If you were to die unconverted, a rebel against your Father in heaven (if not against your earthly parent), see the bitter tears which would be shed over your lost soul. For God has recorded this one instance as a sample. 2. Surely God himself feels for you, otherwise this would not have been recorded. 3. Ay, and how vehement is his own desire for your soul!

Psa. 139:1-2, 23-24, 'O Lord, thou hast searched me and known me. Thou knowest mine downsitting and mine uprising; thou understandest my thought afar off . . . Search me, O God, and know my heart; try me and know my thoughts; and see if there be any wicked way in me; and lead me in the way everlasting.'

Rom. 2:5. 'The day of wrath.'

Job 36:18. 'Because there is wrath, beware lest he take thee away with a stroke; then, a great ransom cannot deliver thee.'

> 1. Health did not prove that you were never to be sick; so the present time of quiet does not prove that there is no day of wrath. 2. There is wrath for sin and sinners. 3. You may be cut off suddenly. 4. If once away, no ransom can deliver you. 5. There is a great ransom ready now, by which you may be saved.

James 2:10-11. 'For whosoever shall keep the whole law, and yet offend in one point, he is guilty of all. For he that said, Do not commit adultery, said also, Do not kill.'

> However outwardly blameless you have been, yet your *heart-sins* bring you in guilty; for he has said, 'Thou shalt love the Lord thy God with all thy heart, and all thy soul, and all thy mind, and all thy strength.' Hast thou done this?

Mark 7:32-33. 'And they bring to him one that was deaf and had an impediment in his speech, and beseech him to put his hand upon him. And he took him aside from the multitude.'

> 1. Notice; just as you have been laid aside from your ordinary employment, and your companions, this man is led aside from the busy gazing crowd. 2. This is done that he may be alone with Jesus, and feel himself in the hands of Jesus.

2 Kings 6:15, 17. 'Alas! my master, how shall we do! . . . And Elisha prayed and said, Lord, I pray thee, open his eyes that he may see! And the Lord opened the eyes of the young man, and he saw.'

> In a time of danger and fear, God kindly showed this young man what help Elisha had at hand in his God. He may show *you* at such a time what help his people find in their God and Saviour.'

Psa. 119:37. 'Turn away mine eyes from beholding vanity.'

Psa. 27:8. 'When thou saidst, Seek ye my face; my heart said unto thee, Thy face, Lord, will I seek.'

> 1. Is he not so speaking to you in this time of trouble? What, then, is your answer? 2. *Jesus* reveals him; see God in seeing Jesus; know his thoughts by knowing Jesus; learn your warrant for expecting favour, by learning what he thinks of the work of Jesus for sinners.

2 Cor. 5:10. 'For we must all appear before the judgment-seat of Christ, that everyone may receive the things done in the body, according to what he hath done, whether it be good or bad.'

Eccles. 11:9. 'Rejoice, O young man, in thy youth, and let thy heart cheer thee in the days of thy youth; and walk in the ways of thy heart, and in the sight of thine eyes:—but know, for all these things God will bring thee into judgment.'

John 4:13. 'Whosoever drinketh of this water shall thirst again.'

> Earth's best pleasures cannot fill the soul. In spite of them it is thirst! thirst again! But John 6:35, says, 'He that believeth on me shall never thirst.' The thirst of the soul is removed when Christ is found.

Lam. 3:27-29. 'It is good for a man that he bear the yoke in his youth. He sitteth alone and keepeth silence because he hath borne it upon him. He putteth his mouth in the dust, if so be there may be hope.'

> 1. God has sent this trouble; submit: 'Where one tear falls

from complying with God's will, a hundred fall in conse-
quence of having our own.'—*Grosvenor*. 2. From the depth
of a pit, at noonday, men see the stars; so you may discover
God's salvation when you are brought very low.

1 Pet. 4:3. 'The time past of our life may suffice us to
have wrought the will of the Gentiles.'

1 John 2:14. 'I have written unto you, young men,
because ye are strong, and the word of God abideth in
you, and ye have overcome the wicked one.'

> 1. See what young men may attain to : Like the three youths
> cast into Nebuchadnezzar's furnace (*Dan.* 3), you may be
> ready to meet death fearlessly, as well as overcome Satan.
> How? If the '*word of God abide in you*'. What is this
> word? It is what God tells of your state as a sinner, and
> his provision for your sinful case in Christ Jesus. It is his
> gospel received into our soul, the good news about Christ
> and his work, and the Father's heart of love therein opened
> to view; all which the Comforter will show to your soul.

Acts 21:14. 'We ceased, saying, The will of the Lord
be done.'

> 'If God (says one) were to study a sure way of being
> revenged upon man, he need only open his stores and let
> him *choose for himself*.'

Matt. 18:8-9. 'Wherefore, if thy hand, or thy foot,
offend thee, cut them off and cast them from thee. It is
better for thee to enter into life halt or maimed, rather than
having two hands or two feet, to be cast into everlasting

fire. And if thine eye offend thee, pluck it out . . .'

> Perhaps God has by this sickness come to cut off the foot
> or pluck out the eye that made thee sin. Consider this! It
> may lead to the saving of thy soul.

2 Cor. 6:17-18: 'Wherefore, come out from among
them, and be separate, saith the Lord: and touch not the
unclean thing, and I will receive you, and I will be a father
unto you; and ye shall be my sons and daughters, saith
the Lord Almighty.'

> 1. Connect with this invitation, this cordial, urgent, yearn-
> ing invitation, the *Parable of the Prodigal Son,* in Luke
> 15. Is it not as if the Father had sent out messengers to
> seek his son, and had sent them to the very swine-troughs
> over which his poor son was wistfully bending, to bid him
> remember the provision of his father's house, assuring him
> at the same time of a most cordial welcome in spite of all
> the past follies of his youth? 2. By sickness, is not the Lord
> sending 'a mighty famine' on you, to drive you out of the
> world and send you to this home?

Judg. 17:13. 'Then said Micah, Now I know that
the Lord will do me good, seeing I have a Levite to my
priest.'

> Beware of being like this young man. He rested on a false
> foundation. He spoke peace to himself when God had
> not done it; for he was resting on a self-made priest, and
> a human religion, instead of using God's one sacrifice of
> atonement. Can you say, 'Now I know that the Lord will

do me good', because of what you have found in the Lord Jesus? (2 *Tim.* 1:12).

INTRODUCTION TO CHAPTER 15

FOR CHILDREN WHO ARE SICK

The Lord, who by his Spirit 'opened the heart of Lydia' so that she 'attended to the things spoken by Paul' (*Acts* 16:14), is the Lord whom we need to accompany us in dealing with children. The Father's drawings, and the Spirit's inward, supernatural, converting work, are as necessary in the case of the youngest child as in the case of the oldest Manasseh. Attention of the right sort is rare among such souls when you are dealing with them about spiritual things, such as sin, conversion, salvation.

1. Speak directly to their *conscience*. Tell them of their inexcusable sin. How daring it is in even little children to dispute the will of the Holy One! Use *texts* of the Bible.

2. Declare the gospel to them as you would to the old. 'He has revealed these things to *babes*', — babes in age or

in understanding. Let us proceed in some such way as this. Take up Isaiah 53:6, 'We all like sheep have gone astray.' *a*. Here is the case of the youngest—'we *all*'. *b*. And then, 'every one after *his own way*'. Here is the special sins of children, *your own* way. You have a way of forgetting God, different from other people, but a way that is as really leading you from God. What is to become of such poor, silly wanderers? Such stubborn, selfish, wilful, worldly ones? *c*. There is here, however, a return pointed out for you. 'The Lord laid on *him* the iniquity of us all.' Tell of the Lord Jesus; how every sin of every one who was ever saved has been laid on him; and tell that this is the only escape for the youngest. *d*. And press their *immediate* return. Remind them of their Shepherd's heart of love, as in John 10:11. *e*. And here, sometimes speak of Christ having been a child—'the child Jesus'. Tell of his expressing his sympathy, and showing his deep, deep interest in children; for he was a child, that he might save a child.

3. It is good occasionally to direct attention to the experience of other children saved by grace, such as we find in *Janeway's Token for Children*.

4. Expect to see fruit of such visits. 'Have ye never read, Out of the mouth of babes and sucklings thou hast perfected praise?' (*Matt.* 21:16).

15

FOR CHILDREN WHO ARE SICK

Mark 5:23. 'My little daughter lieth at the point of death.' Verse 41. 'And Jesus took the damsel by the hand, and said unto her, Talitha-cumi! which is, being interpreted, Damsel (I say unto thee), Arise!'

> She was only twelve years old. See, 1. How Jesus cares for such as you on a bed of sickness, or of death. 2. How He put forth his power over the grave in behalf of one like you. 3. Would you be afraid to commit your soul to one who spoke so kindly?

Eccles. 11:10. 'Remove sorrow from thy heart, and put away evil from thy flesh: for childhood and youth are vanity.'

> You are feeling that childhood is vanity; it has brought you sorrow. Well, put away this evil and sorrow. 'But tell me how?' Surely, by taking God's way of washing out sin, and of wiping away tears. 'But what is that way?' You know Christ Jesus, what he is and what he did? Believing

in him, who so 'bore our sins on his own body on the tree', is the way.

Eccles. 12:1. 'Remember now thy Creator in the days of thy youth, while the evil days come not . . .'

> The evil days have already come on you; nevertheless, 'Remember thy Creator', *i.e.* remember what he is, and what he has done for you. Remember how, since Solomon's days, he has 'sent his Son to be the propitiation for our sins'. Remember his call, 'Come unto me.'

Exod, 16:21. 'And they gathered the manna every morning, every man according to his eating: and when the sun waxed hot, it melted.'

> You know the manna was a type of Christ, who is bread to our souls. Now notice, 1. It was to be gathered very early; and so should you find Christ, and have him as your soul's food, very young. 2. It melted like snow, if not taken early; and so Christ will be out of your reach, if you do not take him soon. 3. Your sickness is like the 'sun waxing hot'; for it may soon take you away from the earth, and then you are away for ever from Christ, if you have not found him before.

Isa. 53:6. 'All we, like sheep, have gone astray; we have turned everyone to his own way.'

John 10:11. 'I am the good shepherd: the good shepherd giveth his life for the sheep.'

John 10:9. 'I am the door: by me if any man enter in he shall be saved.'

John 6:37. 'Him that cometh unto me, I will in no wise cast out.'

> No, not though you be coming now only because sickness has stopped you in your carelessness.

John 3:36. 'The wrath of God!'
Psa. 32:7. 'Thou art my hiding-place.'

> 1. You need a hiding-place. 2. Your sickness tells you that you must find it quickly. 3. God in Christ, not imputing unto men their trespasses, is the hiding-place you need. See verses 1-2.

Jer. 8:22. 'Is there no balm in Gilead? Is there no physician there?'

> 1. You are sick with sin. 2. Christ is the cure, 'the balm, the medicine. 3. Christ also is the physician, who applies his cure by his Holy Spirit.

> *Life is short, and death is sure:*
> *Sin's the wound, and Christ's the cure.*

Luke 19:10. 'The Son of man is come to seek and to save that which is lost.'

Rev. 1:7. 'Every eye shall see him!'

> You shall see him, however young you be. 1. You may see him soon, if you die, in the other world. 2. You will soon see him coming again. 3. Can you say, Lo! there is *my* Saviour?

Ezek. 18:20. 'The soul that sinneth it shall die.'

Rom. 5:12. 'Death by sin.'

> 1. Sickness and the death of the body come by sin. 2. Wrath and hell come by sin. 3. Even one sin brings death. 4. You must be cleansed from *all* sin.

Matt. 16:26. 'What shall a man give in exchange for his soul.'[1]

Luke 15:32. 'It was meet that we should make merry, and be glad: for this thy brother was dead, and is alive again; and was lost, and is found.'

Psa. 50:15. 'Call upon me in the day of trouble.'

> Did not Peter cry to Christ when sinking. 1. Is your body in trouble? Call on him for relief, for Christ's sake. 2. Is your soul also troubled? Call on him, and at the same time look where he looks, namely, at Christ's obedience and death in our place.

1 Kings 14:1, 12-13. 'At that time Abijah the son of Jeroboam fell sick . . . The child shall die, and all Israel shall mourn for him and bury him; for he only of Jeroboam shall come to the grave, because in him there is found some good thing toward the Lord God of Israel in the house of Jeroboam.'

---

[1] 'Turn back and save me, and I will give you £30,000', cried a passenger on board a vessel that was going to pieces, as one of the boats was moving off. The boat turned back. But before it reached the man, he had sunk! We are told of another who, just as he was dying, began to see that his soul was not saved, and cried out, 'Ten thousand worlds for an inch of time!'

For Children who are Sick

1. Abijah was a child of God. 2. The 'good thing toward the Lord' found in him, was saving faith, his soul believing in the Lord, and not resting in idols, or earthly things. He was a young believer. 3. His father, mother, and friends believed that the golden calves were as good for putting away sin as the *sacrifice on the Lord's altar;* but Abijah trusted only in the Lord's sacrifice. 4. He died early, because God wished to take him soon out of the midst of the evil that was around him.[2]

2 Kings 4:18-21. 'And when the child was grown, it fell on a day, that he went out to his father to the reapers; and he said unto his father, My head! my head! And he said to a lad, Carry him to his mother. And when he had taken him, and brought him to his mother, he sat on her knees till noon, and then died! And she went up and laid him on the bed of the man of God, and shut the door upon him, and went out.' Then at verse 33-34, 'Elisha prayed unto the Lord, and stretched himself upon the child', till, verse 35, 'The child sneezed seven times, and the child opened his eyes.'

1. Every little circumstance in this boy's sickness and death is carefully told, to show God's care over the young,—his playing among the reapers, the pain in his head, the lad carrying him, his sitting on his mother's knee, *etc.* Then,

[2] As you think on Abijah may you not say—
I see a lamb within that fold
To which there is an open door
For him, and me, and thousands more?

2. The Lord brought him back to life, as he did the son of the widow of Sarepta (*1 Kings* 17:23), showing his power and his willingness to deliver from death, when it is for his glory. 3. Would not that boy feel himself entirely the Lord's, soul and body? 4. How would you live, if you had once been dead, and had seen heaven and hell? Perhaps you think, 'Oh, I would surely live for the Lord, then.' But Christ says, that if, with your Bible telling all this, you do not now live for him, neither would you be persuaded to do so then (*Luke* 16:31). 5. The Holy Spirit must bless to you what you now know and see, if ever you are to be saved.

John 1:29. 'Behold the Lamb of God! which taketh away the sin of the world.'

Think of the fact of your having sin; of the *fault* or guilt of it; of the *folly* of it. Think of the *fountain* of it, viz., your original sin; think of the *fruit* of it—death.—*M. Henry.* Surely you need the Lamb of God.

Rev. 7:13-14. 'What are these which are arrayed in white robes? . . . These are they which came out of great tribulation, and have washed their robes, and made them white in the blood of the Lamb.'

Young people are among them; perhaps some of those mentioned, Matt. 21:15, who cried to Christ, 'Hosanna', *i.e.* Save us, we pray. Well—1. They suffered much. 2. They got safe through their suffering. 3. It was not their suffering that made them white; it was 'the blood of the Lamb'. 4. How did they wash? They used to believe, think upon, and speak to God, about Christ having poured out his life for sinners.

For Children who are Sick

Mark 9:17-18, 21-22. 'Master, I have brought unto thee my son, which hath a dumb spirit, and wheresoever he taketh him, he teareth him, and he foameth, and gnasheth with his teeth, and pineth away. And he asked his father, How long is it ago since this came unto him? And he said, Of a child; and ofttimes it hath cast him into the fire, and into the waters to destroy him. But if thou canst do anything, have compassion on us and help us.' Jesus, verse 25, 'rebuked the foul spirit, saying unto him, Thou dumb and deaf spirit, I charge thee come out of him, and enter no more into him.'

> 1. See the devil's cruelty, how gladly he would destroy soul and body. 2. See Christ's compassion for this young person.

2 Sam 12:15. 'And God struck the child, and it was very sick.'

> 1. God sends sickness. 2. Even an infant's sin deserves sickness and death.

2 Thess. 1:8-9. '. . . vengeance on them that know not God, and that obey not the gospel of our Lord Jesus Christ; who shall be punished with everlasting destruction.'

> Eternal punishment, Matt. 25:41, 46, is due to the youngest sinner, because sin is so great an evil; for nobody asks about the time taken to commit crime, but only, Was it done? A murder may be done in a moment.

Psa. 106:4. 'Remember me, O Lord, with the favour that thou beareth unto thy people. O visit me with thy salvation.'

Eph. 2:14. 'He is our peace.'

> Christ is, 1. The maker of it, and the means of bringing it to us. 2. All God's reasons for being at peace with a sinner are to be found in Christ.

Isa. 45:24. 'In the Lord I have righteousness.'

Rom. 10:4. 'Christ is the end of the law for righteousness to every one that believeth.' And, Phil. 3:9 '. . . the righteousess which is of God by faith.'

> Let me think on—1. The fact that God has provided righteousness in Christ for the unrighteous. 2. The fountain of that righteousness. It is 'of God'. 3. The freeness of it—it is unto all that believe. 4. The fulness—it must be immense, for it is the righteousness of God-man. 5. The finding of it—it is found by faith. 6. The fruit of it—eternal life.

Psa. 6:2. 'O Lord, heal me, for my bones are vexed.'

> *In life's gay prime a thousand joys I sought,*
> *But heaven and my immortal soul forgot.*
> *In riper days, affliction's smarting rod,*
> *And deep decline, taught me to know my God:*
> *The change I blessed with my expiring breath,*
> *And life ascribed to that which brought me death.*
> —Basil Wood.

Introduction to Chapter 16

For Those Attending to the Sick

When we have opportunity, let us, in visiting, say to the attendants such things as the following:—

1. The Holy Spirit may keep you from being like sextons, who can bury the dead without a serious thought; the Holy Spirit can make to you this sick-room a place for getting and giving instruction. *a*. He is the 'Spirit of counsel and might' (*Isa.* 11:2)—the Spirit who suggests advice, and who enables the hearer to receive it. *b*. He is the Spirit of 'the fear of the Lord'; who can enable you always to realise the Lord's presence and the Lord's doings, in that room.

2. You have a twofold duty. The *first* is—to embrace opportunities of dropping a word in season, just as you would hasten to convey a cordial, or a medicine, or any refreshment. A word, a text, may be blessed. Remember

Naaman's little maid. The *second* is—to attend to your own souls; to seek to be profited. You are warned by this sight. Oh how deep will the arrow of remorse pierce, if after this you be found unprepared. 'Who among you will give heed to this? Who will hearken and give ear for the time to come?' (*Isa.* 42:23).

As visitors, it will be our part to speak of these things; and we can do this very effectually oftentimes, nay, almost always, by leaving with them some such seasonable text as is given in this chapter. Only, let it not be a matter of form; the text must flow from our own heart's fulness.

And let us pray for them. Do as those did, 1 Sam. 30:11, who found the poor sick Egyptian lad: 'They brought him to David'; and David gave him bread and water, figs and raisins. Our David will not be less compassionate and liberal.

16

FOR THOSE ATTENDING TO THE SICK

Rom. 12:6, 8. 'Having then gifts, differing according to the grace that is given unto us, ... he that sheweth mercy [let him do it], with cheerfulness.'

> Waiting on the sick is 'showing mercy'. A Christian does this without fretting, cheerful in his own soul, and cheering others.

2 Tim. 1:16. 'The Lord give mercy to the house of Onesiphorus, for he oft refreshed me, and was not ashamed of my chain.'

> See him visiting Paul in the cold, damp prison. In return, his reward is 'mercy' to himself and family at the day of the Lord.

Luke 10:34. '[A certain Samaritan] went to him, and bound up his wounds, pouring in oil and wine, and set him on his own beast, and brought him to an inn and took care of him.'

Our Lord describes this Samaritan as 'he that showed mercy on his neighbour', verse 37; and says, 'Go and do thou likewise.'

Phil. 4:18. 'I have received of Epaphroditus the things which were sent from you, an odour of a sweet smell, a sacrifice acceptable, well-pleasing to God.'

1. See how very acceptable to God is a small kindness done to a suffering saint. If done *as unto Christ,* lo! it has all the sweet savour of the sacrifice around it. 2. Lay your patient attentions to the sick on the altar before God.

Acts 15:25. 'And the prisoners heard them.'

Would you not have liked to hear the prayers and praises of these afflicted saints? It may be, you are sent to that sick-bed to hear something of a like kind.

Mark 10:45. 'The Son of man came not to be ministered unto, but to minister.'

Luke 22:27. 'I am among you as he that serves.'

Set your Lord before you as a pattern. He was like the *servant* in the room. How honourable your office![1]

Psa. 35:13. 'When they were sick, . . . my prayer returned into mine own bosom.'

1. Pray for those you wait upon. 2. If they are hardened, still pray on; you yourself get the answer to your soul, if they do not. 3. In this you are like the Master.

---

[1] 'Binding up wounds is his office.'—*S. Rutherford*. Seek this part of the mind of Christ.

Eccles. 7:2. 'It is better to go to the house of mourning, than to go to the house of feasting.'

> 1. 'The words of the afflicted many times work very efficaciously. They win the heart and slide into your soul.' — *Brooks*. 2. The spectacle of mortality which you witness preaches to you the need of the 'shadow of the Great Rock in the weary land.'

Eccles. 7:2. 'The living will lay it to his heart.'

> That is 'Surely they will!' This is the most likely means of leading the living to serious thought. Compare Mark 12:6. 'They will reverence my Son'; *q.d.* the sending of such a messenger is the best means for producing loving fear.

Matt. 10:42. 'Whosoever shall give a cup of cold water only, in the name of a disciple, Verily, I say unto you, he shall in no wise lose his reward.'

Luke 13:2-3. 'Suppose ye that these Galileans were sinners above all the Galileans, because they suffered such things? I tell you, nay; but except ye repent, ye shall all likewise perish.'

> Learn from the sufferings you witness in others what sin has brought in; and do not suppose *yourself* less deserving of such suffering.[2]

Isa. 13:23. 'Who among you will give ear to this? Who will hearken and hear for the time to come?'

---

[2] 'Let no man think himself the better, because he is more free from troubles than others. God sees him not fit to bear greater.' — *Sibbes' Medit.*

2 Kings 5:13-14. 'And his servants came near and spake unto him, and said, My father, if the prophet had bid thee do some great thing, wouldest thou not have done it? how much rather, then, when he saith to thee, Wash and be clean? Then went he down.'

> 1. Speak respectfully and kindly; it may be you may be of use to the souls of those you wait upon, as Naaman's servants were of use to him. And as also, verse 3, *'the little maid'* was, in her place. 2. Watch for seasonable occasions.

James 1:5. 'If any of you lack wisdom, let him ask of God, who giveth to all men liberally, and upbraideth not, and it shall be given him.'

Heb. 13:3. 'Remember them that are in bonds as bound with them, and them which suffer adversity, as being yourselves also in the body.'

> As he says in Exod. 23:9. 'Ye know the heart of a stranger, seeing ye were strangers in the land of Egypt.'

Eph. 6:6. 'Not with eye-service, as men-pleasers.'

> And again, in another epistle, because of its importance; Col. 3:22. 'Not with eye-service, as men-pleasers.'

Jon. 1:15-16. 'So they took up Jonah and cast him into the sea, and the sea ceased from its raging. Then the men feared the Lord exceedingly, and offered a sacrifice unto the Lord, and made vows.'

You are situated like those mariners; you are witnesses of a storm. What shall be the effect on you?

Psa. 147:3. 'He healeth the broken in heart, and bindeth up their wounds.'

Your attendance on the sick may become an emblem, and should be a copy, of the Lord's tenderness.

Job 23:23-24. 'If there be a messenger with him, an interpreter, one among a thousand, to shew unto man his uprightness, then is he gracious unto him, and saith, Deliver from going down to the pit; I have found a ransom.'

1. The language of this verse is taken from a sick-room. The sick man is described at verses 19-22. Now, the drift of the passage is this: Suppose there be beside him one who brings God's message, and interprets God's will to that sick man, whose sin has found him out, this may be the means of the sick man's deliverance, soul and body. 2. Though you be the instrument, Christ is 'the *Messenger*' in reality; Christ is the '*Interpreter*', who reveals God, and stands between God and man; Christ is that *rare One*, who shows to us God's righteousness. 3. Your part is to speak of this Saviour, and so bring him into the sick-room. 4. Thus you are the contrast to Hazael (2 *Kings* 8:15), who slew his sick master.

Esther 6:1. 'On that night could not the king sleep, and he commanded to bring the book of records.'

You may have opportunities of bringing forward to the

sick, on a sleepless night, the records of God's Son.

John 4:51, 53. 'And as he was now going down, his servants met him, and told him, saying, Thy son liveth. Then inquired he of them the hour when he began to amend; and they said, Yesterday, at the seventh hour, the fever left him . . . And himself believed, and his whole house.'

> Blessed sickness! all the servants are blessed thereby, and all the family.

Matt. 25:36. 'Sick, and ye visited me.' Verse 39. 'When saw we thee sick?' Verse 40. 'Inasmuch as ye did it unto one of the least of these my brethren, ye have done it unto me.'

Deut. 29:2-4. 'Ye have seen all that the Lord did before your eyes in the land of Egypt unto Pharaoh and unto all his servants, and unto all his land; the great temptations [events fitted to test and try] which thine eyes have seen, the signs, and those great miracles; yet the Lord hath not given you an heart to perceive, and eyes to see, and ears to hear, unto this day.'

> Halyburton on his deathbed said to the attending physician, 'Sir, I give you solemn warning, that if you become hardened by the frequent sight of sick and dying persons, you will be in danger of losing all sensibility of conscience, and being hardened for ever.'

For Those Attending to the Sick

Servant of all, to toil for man
Thou didst not, Lord, refuse;
Thy majesty did not disdain
To be employed for us.

Thy bright example I pursue;
To thee in all things rise;
And all I think, or speak, or do,
Is one great sacrifice.

Careless through outward cares I go,
From all distraction free;
My hands are but engaged below,
My heart is still with thee.

—Moravian

Introduction to Chapter 17

For the Friends of the Sick

Some things spoken of in the introduction to the last chapter apply here also. One thing let us remember, *viz.*, we must have the Spirit with us and in us. Stephen was 'full of faith and power' (*Acts* 6:8), so that they could not resist his words; but he was so because 'full of the Holy Ghost', verse 3.

1. Let us counsel the friends of the sick not to speak so to undo what the minister, or other visitor, may have said. Friends must beware of speaking lightly at the bedside of the sick. An old writer (Swinnock) says on this point, 'Hazael's wet cloth was not more deadly to his master's body, than the discourse of most is to their sick neighbours' souls.'

2. Let us encourage the friends of the sick not to be moved by the fear of displeasing the sick, but to be

faithful to them. O beware of sewing pillows for dying men's souls!

3. Let us remind them, that this may be their time, their tide-time, for being of use to the sick person's soul.

4. Let us remind the friends, that if they are not taking pains with the soul of their sick ones, these souls may be lost. And if they are lost, may these lost not say to such friends hereafter (as an old writer suggests), 'Sir, if thou hadst been there to speak to me for Christ, my soul had not died'?

5. Let us tell Christ about our sick; as Mark 10:39. It is a time for prayer, Zech. 10:1; Jer. 33:3.

6. Let us remind friends that they are expected to learn by their neighbours' trials.

The texts quoted in the chapter may help us in all the above particulars, not forgetting to mingle prayer in the name of Jesus; for it is written, 'I beseech you the rather to do this, that I may be restored to you the sooner' (*Heb.* 13:19).

17

FOR THE FRIENDS OF THE SICK

Mark 1:30. 'Simon's wife's mother lay sick of a fever; and anon they tell him of her.'

Matt. 8:5-6. 'There came unto him a centurion, beseeching him, and saying, Lord, my servant lieth at home sick of the palsy, grievously tormented. And Jesus saith unto him, I will come and heal him.'

Mark 2:3, 5. 'They come unto him, bringing one sick of the palsy, which was borne of four . . . When Jesus saw their faith, he said unto the sick of the palsy, Son, thy sins are forgiven thee.'

> 1. Friends ought to lay before Jesus their sick friends. 2. Jesus is pleased at this. 3. Jesus had respect to the faith of the *friends,* as well as the sick man's, in giving the cure.

Philm. 22. 'I trust that through your prayers I shall be given unto you.'

John 11:3. 'Therefore his sisters sent unto him, saying, Lord, he whom thou lovest is sick.'

Matt. 15:22. 'Behold a woman of Canaan came out of the same coasts and cried unto him, saying, Have mercy on me, O Lord, thou son of David, my daughter is grievously vexed with a devil.'

> 1. This woman feels that the daughter's recovery would be mercy to her mother also. 2. She feels she has no claim, or right to insist on a cure; 'mercy! mercy!'

Phil. 2:27. 'God had mercy on him, and not on him only, but on me also; lest I should have sorrow upon sorrow.'

> 1. You do not deserve to be spared this sorrow. 2. Ask the deliverance merely as an undeserved 'mercy'. 3. The Lord does not wish to afflict you. He would gladly spare you 'sorrow upon sorrow'; he grieves to see tear chasing tear down your cheek. 4. He may make your friend an Epaphroditus, raised up again.

2 Kings 13:14-15. 'Now Elisha was fallen sick of his sickness whereof he died; and Joash the king of Israel came down unto him, and wept over his face, and said, O my father, my father! the chariot of Israel and the horsemen thereof. And Elisha said unto him, Take bow and arrows . . .'

> 1. Joash lamented the prospect of the prophet's death as if it were equivalent to losing Israel's best protection, Israel's war chariots. 2. The dying prophet directs his friend, by a symbolical action, to look to the Lord for victory.

3. The God of Elisha lives to be the strength of those who survive Elisha.

Num. 23:10. 'Let me die the death of the righteous, and let my last end be like his!'[1]

> If you witness a scene that draws forth this desire, then remember in that hour the Lord is saying to you what he said in Luke 14:15, 17. When one exclaimed, 'Blessed is he that shall eat bread in the kingdom of God'; Jesus spoke a parable, the point of which was, 'Come, for all things are now ready!'

Psa. 37:37. 'Mark the perfect man and behold the upright, for the end of that man is peace!'

Psa. 90:12. 'So teach us to number our days!'

Job 24:23. 'He will not lay upon man more than is right.'

2 Sam. 12:16. 'David therefore besought God for the child; and David fasted, and went in and lay all night upon the earth.' Then, verse 22. 'He said, While the child was yet alive I fasted and wept; for I said, Who can tell whether God will be gracious to me, that the child may live?'

> 1. In matters of this kind we know not God's will, and so we pray, saying, 'Who can tell?' 2. But we are not to prescribe to God the nature of the answer to our prayer.

1 Pet. 5:6. 'Humble yourselves under the mighty hand of God, that he may exalt you in due time.'

---

[1] 'Nothing is a more powerful means of making young [and old] persons think, than the sight of sanctified affliction.'—*Love's Letters*.

James 5:16. 'Confess your faults one to another, and pray one for another, that you may be healed.'

> As you think it right for a nation to confess sin, in order that the public calamity may be removed; so also a family and friends ought to do.

Job 19:17. 'Have pity upon me, have pity upon me, O my friends, for the hand of God has touched me.'

1 Cor. 12:26. 'Whether one member suffer, all the members suffer with it; or one member be honoured, all the members rejoice with it.'

> This is the happy law of the household of faith; and applies to Christ the Head also!

Matt. 15:30-31. 'Great multitudes came unto him, having with them those that were lame, blind, dumb, maimed, and many others, and cast them down at Jesus' feet, and he healed them, insomuch that the multitude wondered . . . And they glorified the God of Israel.'

Luke 7:16. 'And there came a fear upon all, and they glorified God.'

> 1. The result of God's dealing in these cases of distress was *glory to his name*. 2. It was the standers-by who thus glorified him.

Rev. 9:13. 'The remnant were affrighted, and gave glory to the God of heaven.'

Acts 9:5-6. 'It is hard for thee to kick against the pricks . . . Lord, what wilt thou have me to do?'

1. When subjected to the anguish of seeing friends sick or dying, do not fret at God. The ox that kicked at the sharp-pointed goad only made itself bleed. 2. Ask rather; Lord, what is all this to teach me?

Psa. 61:2. 'When my heart is overwhelmed, lead me to the Rock that is higher than I.'

Higher than Satan, than self, than sorrow's flood. Let me be under the shadow of that Rock, or in one of its clefts.

Song of Sol. 1:7. 'Tell me, O thou whom my soul loveth, where thou feedest, where thou makest thy flock to rest at noon.'

Isa. 38:1. 'In those days was Hezekiah sick unto death: and Isaiah the prophet, the son of Amoz, came unto him and said, Set thine house in order; for thou shalt die, and not live.'

1. Friends must speak truthfully to sick friends, and tell the sick the real danger of their case. 2. They must remind them of what is preparation for death. 3. Isaiah did this to a king. 4. Preparation is having part in Christ.

Job 11:13-15. 'If thou prepare thine heart, and stretch out thine hands toward him; if iniquity be in thine hand, put it far away, and let not wickedness dwell in thy tabernacles. For then shalt thou lift up thy face without spot; yea, thou shalt be stedfast, and shalt not fear.'

1. This is a friend's advice to one whom he thought unprepared to meet God. Zophar was wrong in his view of Job's case, but at any rate he was faithful to him so far

as his light went. 2. Go and do likewise. 3. Zophar gives a true view of real preparation, *viz.,* the heart set right toward God, bent on finding forgiving mercy, peace of conscience, acceptance found, sanctification begun.

Job 22:21-24. 'Acquaint now (*i.e.* I pray thee) thyself with him and be at peace; thereby good shall come unto thee. Receive, I pray thee, the law from his mouth, and lay up his words in thine heart. If thou return to the Almighty, thou shalt be built up: thou shalt put away iniquity far from thy tabernacles. Then thou shalt lay up gold as dust.'

> 1. Here is another faithful friend, up to the measure of his light as to Job's case. 2. His counsel is just such as you should give to your sick friend. 3. How kindly he speaks: 'I pray thee! I pray thee!'

Job 33:1. 'Wherefore, Job, I pray thee, hear my speeches, and hearken to all my words.'

> 1. This is Elihu speaking to his friend. In so doing, he tells of the 'messenger', the 'interpreter' (33:23); he tells of God's purpose in affliction (36:8); he tells much of God's character and ways, wishing to bring his friend to a right state of soul. 2. Go and do likewise.

Psa. 41:1. 'Blessed is he that considereth the poor.' [The reduced one—reduced by poverty, or by trouble.]

PART III

THE WORD BROUGHT NEAR
TO THE SORROWFUL

Introduction to Chapter 18

The Sorrowful, when Their Thoughts Are Directed to Their own Loss in the Death of Friends

Let us call to mind that name of the Spirit, '*The Comforter*', for it is one who, in comforting, exhorts, stirs up, pleads in us for God. It is such a one as this that we need to have with us to give power to our words; otherwise the sorrowful will remain sorrowful. Let us remember, too, Christ (*Isa.* 61:2) is sent 'to *comfort*'; so that we have him as at once our subject and our guide. And the Father (2 *Thess.* 2:16) giveth '*everlasting consolation*' by the Spirit, through the Son.

Such thoughts of God being in our heart, we go forth, assured that our God desires us to relieve the sorrowing. 'I saw the tents of Cushan in affliction' (*Hab.* 3:7): who reads this and does not feel his eye turn thither sympathisingly?

1. Meeting those who feel *left alone* in the world, our great aim is to set before them the Lord Jesus Christ, in order that they may never be alone, while they have a living Christ, in the fulness of sympathy, power, grace:—a living Christ who may be father, mother, sister, friend, son, daughter, husband, wife—all in all.

2. If the persons are *not in Christ* already, of course our great aim is to introduce to their notice that *which alone fills the soul.* We tell them of *him and his salvation.*

3. Be careful to speak no comfort about Christ's presence, or the like, to those *out of Christ.* At the same time be careful to tell such souls of the rich comfort *awaiting them,* if now they receive Christ into the place left empty by their bereavement.

4. Pray fervently, as those who do 'weep with those that weep.'

5. Try to engage the bereaved themselves to *pray* also, when you have left them. '*To act* in trouble is to blunt its edge.'

6. Give them some short text at parting, that may sink into their soul. Such texts have been called, 'A cool breeze for a burning brow.'

7. An old writer (Swinnock) says, 'It is good manners to be an unbidden guest in the house of mourning.' If so, how much more may we expect the response of welcome when we are bidden and are looked for?

18

THE SORROWFUL, WHEN THEIR THOUGHTS ARE DIRECTED TO THEIR OWN LOSS IN THE DEATH OF FRIENDS

Heb. 12:11. 'No chastening for the present seemeth to be joyous, but grievous: nevertheless afterward it yieldeth the peaceable fruit of righteousness unto them which are exercised hereby.'

This text was noticed Part 2:1., but it is worth being again considered. 1. *'Fruit of righteousness'*, *i.e.* your being made more like him who is righteous, and made to cling more to him as your righteousness, from sense of utter weakness and worthlessness. Of this, the result is *'peace'*, as Isa. 32:17 declares. 2. They who are *'exercised'* are those who pass through this exercise who descend into this arena by God's direction. It is an unfettered promise to the true children of God, stating to them that it is God's unvarying custom to bring a harvest from this sad seed-time. Nor does he hamper this promise by saying, 'If you properly feel what you suffer', or, 'If you are in good frame during the time of trouble', 'If you examine yourself', &c. No; *'exercised'* has the simple meaning of 'made to pass through this form of discipline', this spiritual wrestling. It is like passing through the furnace to get quit of the dross.

Ruth 1:20-21. 'The Almighty hath dealt very bitterly with me . . . The Almighty hath afflicted me.'

Naomi's faith shines out from her sadness. Like the Master's 'My God', while asking, 'Why hast thou forsaken me?' So the disciple here. The sap of the vine appears in the bruised branch. 1. 'The Almighty' is *'Shaddai'*, the 'All-sufficient One'. 2. He who thus bereaves is able to support you under the stroke. 3. He who thus empties you of the creature is himself the object that is to take the creature's place and fill your heart. 'I will welcome the pruning-knife', said Luther.

Psa. 37:8. 'Seek ye my face.'

Idols have fallen; cisterns are broken; seek *me!*

John 20:13, 15. 'And they [angels] say unto her, Woman, why weepest thou? . . . Jesus saith unto her, Woman, why weepest thou? Whom seekest thou?'

Unsuffering angels were sent to express sympathy. But the 'man of sorrows' soon came himself to tell his pity, and to wipe tears away with his own hand.

John 11:35. 'Jesus wept.'

1. You know what weeping is (said Dr Wright of Stirling); you know who Jesus is. Well, 'Jesus wept'! 2. Unspeakable condescension here! Such sympathy, such compassion!

even while hastening to remove the cause of sorrow by speedy resurrection. 3. So still; he is to raise his sleeping saints soon. 'Thy brother shall rise again'—yet even now, in the interim, he pours his balsam on thy wound; for this is a balsam, *viz.*, *he* feels for *thee*.

Gen. 23:2-4, 19. 'Abraham came to mourn for Sarah, and to weep for her. And Abraham stood up from before his dead, and spake unto the sons of Heth, saying, I am a stranger and sojourner with you: give me a possession of a burying-place with you, that I may bury my dead out of my sight . . . And after this Abraham buried Sarah his wife in the cave of Machpelah, before Mamre: the same is Hebron in the land of Canaan.'

> 1. Here is deep feeling for a fellow-pilgrim's death. 2. Here is the pilgrim-feeling intensified; anew he confesses that he is but a stranger here. 3. Here is *faith* as well as *feeling;* for therefore it is he buries Sarah in Canaan. He believes the word of the Lord about that land, and he looks forward to resurrection by him who is to be revealed there. 4. These are the accompaniments of the *first funeral* mentioned in the Bible.

Hab. 3:17-19. 'Though the fig-tree shall not blossom, neither shall fruit be in the vines; the labour of the olive shall fail, and the fields shall yield no meat; the flock shall be cut off from the fold, and there shall be no herd in the stall; yet will I rejoice in the Lord; I will joy in the God of my salvation.[1] The Lord God is my strength; and he will make my feet like hinds' feet, and he will make me to walk upon mine high places.'

Ezek. 20:26. 'That I might make them desolate, to the end they might know that I am the Lord.'

1 John 1:7. 'The blood of Jesus Christ, his Son, cleanseth us from all sin.'

> 1. There is strange power in the applied blood of Jesus to give comfort, as well as to give rest from guilt. Think upon it. 2. That blood removes every barrier in the way of God's outpoured love; so that with the blood applied, love comes! 3. Love itself ('God is love') draws near to bathe your soul when you meditate on the outpoured blood of Jesus.

Rom. 5:1-3, 5. 'Being justified by faith, we have peace with God through our Lord Jesus Christ, . . . and rejoice in hope of the glory of God; and not only so, but we glory in tribulations . . . because the love of God is shed abroad in our hearts, by the Holy Ghost which is given unto us.'

> 1. Would Elijah, when he knew that he was about to ascend in his fiery chariot be much oppressed by tribulation? And is not a believer who is assured of God's love, somewhat as Elijah was, expecting ascension ere long? 2. This, then, is the way to true consolation — *'justified by faith*, we have peace, and rejoice in hope of glory.' 3. And the Holy Ghost sheds God's love in our hearts, saying to our soul, he who

---

[1] 'His sweet presence eateth out the bitterness of sorrow.' — *S. Rutherford.* 'It is a rule in divinity, that God never takes away comforts from his people, but he gives them better.' — *Sibbes' Meditations.*

loveth thee so well, and whom thou lovest most of all, is still beside thee.

Rom. 8:1. 'There is therefore now no condemnation to them that are in Christ, who walk not after the flesh, but after the Spirit.'

> 1. Being in the ark, the waters of the flood cannot touch thee. Being in Christ, wrath cannot approach thee. 2. Thou art led by the Spirit also; for the Spirit takes by the hand all that are in Christ. 3. If so, be of good cheer. This is not a drop of wrath, but a token of fatherly love, that has come to thee.[2]

Psa. 119:71. 'It is good for me that I have been afflicted, that I might learn thy statutes.'[3]

> Lord, be it thus with me!

Psa. 145:17, 19. 'The Lord is righteous in all his ways, and holy in all his works . . . He will fulfil the desire of them that fear him.'

Psa. 46:10. 'Be still and know that I am God: I will be exalted.'

Psa. 94:12-13. 'Blessed is the man whom thou chastenest, O Lord, and teachest out of thy law; that thou mayest give him rest from the days of adversity.'

---

[2] 'Why should I start at the plough of my Lord, which maketh deep furrows in my soul? I know he purposeth a crop.'—*S. Rutherford.*
[3] 'A good man under affliction is a patient under cure; and we can but congratulate him, though the operation may be very severe.'—*Cecil.*

1. The pardoned man is 'blessed' (*Psa.* 32:1). But the pardoned man who is 'chastened', is doubly blessed; for he is under the process of sanctification. 2. It is a special time for learning God's will, and feeling the power of the Scriptures. 3. This gracious discipline will end in rest.

Job 5:17-18. 'Behold, happy is the man whom God correcteth; therefore, despise not thou the chastening of the Almighty. For he maketh sore and bindeth up; he woundeth, and his hands make whole. In six troubles he shall deliver thee, yea in seven there shall no evil touch thee.'

Job 11:16. 'Thou shalt forget thy misery—remember it as waters that pass away.'

Isa. 26:4. 'In the Lord Jehovah is the Rock of Ages.' [Heb. margin.]

> The Rock of Ages is not vanished, though friends are. We find the Rock that never moves, not in them, but in the Lord Jehovah.

Jer. 33:3. 'Call unto me, and I will answer thee, and shew thee great and mighty things which thou knowest not.'

2 Sam. 12:19-20. 'Is the child dead? And they said, He is dead.[4] Then David arose from the earth, and washed and anointed himself, and changed his apparel, and came

---

[4] 'How canst thou tell if it had been continued longer to thee, but it might have proved the greatest cross? How often have our bosom contents been turned into gall!'—*Brooks.*

into the house of the Lord, and worshipped: then he came to his own house; and when he required, they set bread before him, and he did eat.'

> He explains his conduct in verses 22-23. But, see, 1. His first act, after the stroke has fallen, is to *visit the Lord,* and speak with him over the atoning sacrifice, in his tabernacle. 2. Then he begins domestic duties once more, revived and gladdened by a fresh sense of divine love.

Psa. 115:17-18. The dead praise not the Lord, neither any go down into silence. But we will bless the Lord from this time forth, and for evermore. Praise ye the Lord.' [*Hallelujah!*]

Psa. 91:15. 'He shall call upon me . . . I will be with him in trouble.'

Psa. 138:7. 'Though I walk in the midst of trouble, thou wilt revive me.'

Psa. 50:15. 'Call upon me in the day of trouble; I will deliver thee, and thou shalt glorify me.'

> 1. Ask the Lord to comfort. 2. Expect to be comforted. 3. Expect some results of this stroke, such as shall forward thy holiness or usefulness. It was while the famous John Howard was sitting by the dead body of his wife that the news of the tremendous earthquake at Lisbon reached him, and so affected him that his private grief was absorbed in concern for the many sufferers. From that day his career of benevolence began. He learned to care for others' sorrows, and to cure his own thereby.

Isa. 32:1-2. 'Behold, a king . . . a man shall be as a hiding-place from the wind, and a covert from the tempest, as rivers of waters in a dry place, as the shadow of a great rock in a weary land.'

> 1. Christ is the king; Christ is this 'Man'. 2. The hiding-place is this king, this 'Man', who is full of feeling for you. It is not a mere deliverance; it is a Deliverer. It is not mere comfort; it is a Comforter for you, one who knows your frame 3. The wind and tempest obey him. 4. He will also refresh you and shade you. Are you a mourner not yet saved? *First,* come to him as *a sinner fleeing from wrath.* He hides, he shades; for he gives you what he has *done* and *suffered. Then,* come to him as a *mourner.*

1 Cor. 3:21-22. 'Let no man glory in men, for all things are yours, whether Paul, or Apollos, or Cephas, or the world, life, or death, or things present, or things to come; all are yours.'[5]

Isa. 51:12. 'I, even I, am he that comforteth you.'

2 Kings 4:26. 'It is well.'

> *Who hath the Father and the Son,*
> *May be left, but not alone.*

John 14:23. 'We will come unto him, and make our abode with him.'

Psa. 119:23. 'Princes also did sit and speak against me but thy servant did meditate on thy statutes.'

---

[5] 'I see', said one, who had been sorely bereaved, 'God wishes to have all my heart; and he shall have it!'

'A holy divertisement is the best way to ease the trouble of our thoughts. It is not good to pore upon our sorrow. As the husbandmen, when their ground is overflowed by waters, make ditches and water-furrows to carry it away; so, when our minds and thoughts are overloaded with trouble, it is good to direct them to some other matter.'—*Thomas Manton*. God acted thus with Moses; for we find him saying in Deut. 3:26, '*Speak to me no more of this matter*': and then verses 27-28, '*Go to Pisgah*', and, '*Charge Joshua.*' Be occupied with duties.

Gen. 41:50-51. 'And Joseph called the name of his firstborn *Manasseh* ['causing to forget']; for God, said he, hath made me to forget all my toil, and all my father's house. And the name of the second called he *Ephraim*, for God hath caused me to be fruitful in the land of my affliction.'

It shall be thus in the end. But it may be thus in measure even now.

Introduction to Chapter 19

The Sorrowful, when Their Thoughts Are Directed to the State of Those Who Have Died

Men that pray are the only men that need attempt to carry consolation. We read in Jude 20, of *'praying in the Holy Ghost'*; and surely never have we more need of his presence and power than in *speaking*. If one of our poets has asked, 'Who can pluck from the memory a rooted sorrow?' and has truly said, that generally those who themselves are unwounded fancy it easy to give comfort, we must, on this very account, seek to go forth in the power of the true 'Comforter'. He can teach us to speak a word in season 'to *him that is weary*'.

1. Let us beware of being rash in our comforts. Let us not give away to the unconverted that which is the portion only of God's children.

2. In every case, we are safe in trying to bring the mourner to 'consider the High Priest of our profession', instead of leaving him to dwell too much on his own loss. Whether the person be already a believer, or be one who only assents to the faith, we cannot be wrong in aiming at the result of leading him to supply the place of the lost by *Christ himself.*

3. We may, without entering into details, in such a case as Section 2nd presents (where we are left ignorant of the state in which the departed died), urge on surviving friends decided and sure manifestation of an interest in Christ. This is the best legacy to leave behind them.

In a case like the 3rd Section (where we fear that the departed has perished), let us not harrow the feelings of friends; but let us dwell much on the real relief that is found in turning from 'things seen to things that are not seen', from the terrible abyss, to the bright and glorious throne of God, who himself may fill up the void, and sweep away the ever-vexatious and stunning apprehensions of our heart, by becoming to us, more than ever before, the ocean of holy love that bathes us. The *will of God,* in its aspect towards us, is to be much thought upon. 'Blessed is he that is not offended in me.'

Perhaps Isa. 30:15 furnishes us with a peg on which to hang our words. 'In *returning and rest* shall ye be saved; in *quietness and confidence* shall be your strength.' *a*. We seek to withdraw the saddened one from the sad object. *b*. We do this mainly by presenting the ever-full, the ever-free, the ever-fresh fountain of love and sympathy in the Lord Jesus. 'Return', we say, 'return from your field of dismal thoughts and fears, and rest here.' *c*. We urge it, we press it home. 'Quietly abiding here is your source of strength under this stroke.' *d*. We remind that thirsty, thirsty soul, that the Holy Spirit has often made such times as this his special season of visitation, 'shewing a world by night you never saw by day.' *e*. We use this truth even to the unsaved mourners. For to everyone is the water of life free. Turn from all else to this alone. Christ stands ready to receive the guiltiest, and to receive the guiltiest in the time of their greatest grief. And thus we hold the cup of blessing to their lips. It may be, a sovereign God may use our words.

19

THE SORROWFUL, WHEN THEIR THOUGHTS ARE DIRECTED TO THE STATE OF THOSE WHO HAVE DIED

I. IN REGARD TO THOSE WHO HAVE DIED IN THE LORD

Acts 7:60. 'He fell asleep.'

> *One gentle sigh his fetters breaks;*
> *We scarce can say, 'He's gone',*
> *Before the willing spirit takes*
> *His mansion near the throne.*

Phil. 1:23. '. . . To depart and to be with Christ, which is far better.'

> *This much (and this is all) we know,*
> *They are supremely blest;*
> *Have done with sin, and care, and woe,*
> *And with their Saviour rest.*

1 Thess. 4:13-15, 17-18. 'Sorrow not even as others

that have no hope. For if we believe that Jesus died and rose again, even so *them also* that sleep in Jesus will God bring *with him*. For this we say unto you by the word of the Lord, that we which are alive and remain . . . We which are alive and remain, shall be caught up *together with them* in the clouds, to meet the Lord in the air . . . And so shall we ever be with the Lord. Wherefore, comfort one another with these words.'

> The Father will as surely send Christ the second time, as he did the first. Now, to see Christ in glory might be enough to fill any soul for ever. But in great tenderness, as a token of most delicate attention to our feelings as men and friends, the Lord intimates that he will, when Jesus returns, send back our brethren who sleep in Jesus, in his train, that we may rest and rejoice together. 'We', *i.e.* our friends and we, 'shall be ever with the Lord.'[1]

Luke 16:25. 'Now, he is comforted.'

Luke 23:43. 'Today shalt thou be with me in Paradise.'

2 Cor. 5:8. 'Present with the Lord.'

Phil. 1:21. 'To die is gain.'

> Your friend has suddenly become heir to an infinite estate! Lo! what he has gained! A mansion in the many mansions! The full presence of the Lord! Unbroken fellowship! He

---

[1] 'O what folly, to sit down and weep upon a decree of God! For, who can come behind our Lord to alter or better what he hath decreed and done? It were better to make windows in our prison, and cry, O let the Bridegroom come.'—*S. Rutherford.*

sees God (*Matt.* 5:8). 'He hungers no more, he thirsts no more, nor does the sun light on him, nor any heat.' No more 'death, neither sorrow, nor crying; neither shall there be any more pain'. He sees the King in his beauty! He understands the Priest's intercession in its power, and his sacrifice in its merit! He hears the Prophet tell plainly of the Father. 'Eye has not seen nor ear heard' what he already enjoys.

Isa. 57:2. 'He shall enter into peace. They shall rest on heir beds [couches], each one walking in his uprightness.'

> That is, every one who was a 'walker in uprightness'— walking according to God's rule of salvation—enters into peace from all outward troubles. Nay more; he rests as at a feast, 'on their couches', as Christ represents Lazarus leaning on Abraham's bosom, while Abraham leans on the Lord's.

Rev. 6:11. 'White robes were given unto every one of them, and it was said unto them that they should rest yet for a little season, until . . .'

> 1. Arrayed in an interim transfiguration dress (*Matt.* 17:2), because the time for actual transfiguration of soul and body has not come, they rest at the heavenly feast on their couches. 2. They are taught to cherish the prospect of resurrection, when all their brethren shall be gathered in.

Rev. 14:13. 'I heard a voice from heaven saying unto me, Write, Blessed are the dead which die in the Lord. Yea, saith the Spirit.'

Not the voice of partial friends, but the voice from the Excellent Glory, it would appear; the same voice that cried, 'This is my beloved Son' (*Matt.* 3:17). And the *Comforter's* voice too for the Spirit says, 'Yea.'

John 17:24. 'With me where I am.'

Hereafter, in his kingdom; now, at the right hand where he sits, They are with him who says, 'Till the day break and the shadows flee away, I will get me to the mountain of myrrh, and to the hill of frankincense.' The right hand is the spot where the fragrance of his merits breathes its sweet savour before the Father making it a very mountain of myrrh and hill of incense. (Compare *John* 14:3.) Your friends in Jesus are there.

Rev. 7:15-16. 'They are before the throne of God and serve him day and night in his temple. And he that sitteth on the throne shall dwell among them. They shall hunger no more, neither thirst any more, neither shall the sun light on them, nor any heat.'

And there 'the Lamb shall feed them' as a shepherd; see Song of Sol. 2:16-17, 'He feedeth among the lilies till the day break and the shadows flee away.' The Lamb 'leads them to fountains of water'. And, 'God shall wipe away all tears from their eyes.' The Father himself does this.

1 Cor. 15:22. 'As in Adam all die, so in Christ shall all be made alive.'

1. All who are in Adam's family die. 2. All who are in Christ' family shall arise. 3. Adam's sin brought death to

all his family; so, Christ's meritorious righteousness brings life and resurrection to all his family.

John 14:2-3. 'In my Father's house are many mansions; if it were not so I would have told you. I go to prepare a place for you; and if I go and prepare a place for you I will come again, and receive you unto myself, that where I am there ye may be also.'

II. In Regard to Those of Whose State You Are Ignorant

Job 1:21. 'The Lord gave and the Lord hath taken away; blessed be the name of the Lord.'

> Job thus calmly acquiesces, although we are told at verse 5, that he had fears about them. 'It may be, my sons have sinned and cursed God in their hearts.'

Psa. 39:9. 'I was dumb, I opened not my mouth, because thou didst it.'

> Romaine writes: 'I have no stock of resignation; it is out of myself, laid up in the fulness of Jesus, and while I live upon him, he helps me to kiss the rod.'

Deut. 32:4. 'His work is perfect.'

> 1. His doings in grace are so. 2. His doings in providence are no less so.

Job 35:10. 'Where is God my maker, who giveth songs in the night?'[2]

---

[2] 'Now doth the Lord sing to his children's hearts while he weans them

He can make you sing for joy, even when your night has its darkest clouds, and seems to have lost every star. By what you see of God in his beloved Son, through the Spirit's teaching, grief may be absorbed.

Matt. 11:26. 'Even so, Father, for so it seemed good in thy sight.'

> 1. This was our Master's consolation in view of the 'hiding of these things' from the wise and prudent. 2. Sympathise with him in satisfaction with the Father's sovereign will. 3. In doing so, you are 'learning of him', verse 29, and will get that part of '*rest*' which is found in sanctification. 'Ye shall find rest unto your souls.'

2 Sam. 15:26. 'Behold, here am I; let him do as seemeth good unto him.'

Rom. 11:33. 'O the depth of the riches both of the wisdom and knowledge of God! how unsearchable are his judgments, and his ways past finding out.'

> 1. God knows his own dealing with you, in withholding from you the kind of consolation you thirst for. 2. There is a deep mine of wealth for your soul in this very circumstance.

Psa. 77:13, 19. 'Thy way, O God, is in the sanctuary . . . Thy way is in the sea.'

> That is, 1. He has made no secret of his '*way*' as to our salvation; for the Sanctuary, with its rent veil, discloses it all. 2. He has another way, his '*way*' in providence. *That* is beyond our reach to know. 3. But go thou up from 'the

---

in a dark night of affliction.'—*The Weaned Christian*, by S.S.

sea' to 'the sanctuary'. Bathe thy soul in love seen at the mercy-seat instead of trying to bathe thy weary soul in that sea's unfathomable depths.

1 Sam. 3:18. 'It is the Lord! let him do what seemeth him good.'

John 21:21-22. 'Lord, and what shall this man do? Jesus saith unto him, If I will that he tarry till I come, what is that to thee? Follow thou me.'[3]

1 Pet. 1:25. 'But the word of the Lord endureth for ever; and this is the word which by the gospel is preached unto you.'

> 1. Whatever hope is withered (verse 24), the Lord's word remaineth. 2. The gospel is that word, that never-fading word, the good news of God's love to the sinner in his Son. 3. If you cannot know your friend's state, yet in following Christ, you can see plainly God's heart towards you.

Jer. 31:25. 'I have replenished every sorrowful soul.' Verse 12. 'Their soul shall be as a watered garden.'

> 1. When Israel's tears and sorrows are over, they leave his soul like a watered garden. 2. The Lord's dealing has not failed in any one case. 3. He has always 'replenished' and filled full, making the cup run over. 4. He has revealed to you Christ the beloved Son; will you not, then, believe that kindness is meant, in withholding or withdrawing anything else?

---

[3] 'Learn much of Christ at such an hour. Study him at the grave of Lazarus, John 11; at the gate of Nain, Luke 7; and also within the veil, Rev. 1:18.' — *M'Cheyne.*

Psa. 73:28. 'It is good for me to draw near to God. I have put my trust in the Lord God, that I may declare all thy works.'

> 1. Let me turn from the painful subject of my sorrow to my God. 2. Let me leave my sore anxiety on him, assured that I shall 'declare' these his works of providence with joy and with admiration.[4]

III. IN REGARD TO THOSE OF WHOM YOU FEAR THE WORST

Luke 7:23. 'Blessed is he whosoever is not offended in me.'

> 1. While the Lord gives no account of his ways, he asks you to trust him so far as not to think ill of him in the meantime. 2. He that sent you his own Son, is surely worthy to be treated with confidence in your darkest hour. 3. Say as Du Plessis said, 'I could not have borne this from man, but I can bear it from God.'

Lev. 10:1-3. 'And Nadab and Abihu, the sons of Aaron, took either of them his censer, and put fire therein, and put incense thereon, and offered strange fire before the Lord, which he commanded them not. And there went out fire from the Lord and devoured them; and they died before

---

[4] 'To me it seems that the measure of mourning lessens in proportion to man's nearness to God.'—*Grosvenor*. 'There is no believer that usually hath great trouble, but either when his interest in Christ is hid, or when his enjoyment of Christ is small.'—*Traile*.

the Lord. Then Moses said unto Aaron, This is it that the Lord spake, saying, I will be sanctified in them that come nigh me, and before all the people I will be glorified. And Aaron held his peace.'

> 1. Think of the storm in Aaron's soul. 2. Think of the voice in the midst of it, 'God is glorified, and is teaching others to glorify him!' 3. See the great calm that this produces; 'Aaron held his peace.'

Job 23:8-10. 'Behold, I go forward, but he is not there; and backward, but I cannot perceive him; on the left hand, where he doth work, but I cannot behold him; he hideth himself on the right hand, that I cannot see him. But he knoweth the way that I take! When he has tried me, I shall come forth as gold.'

> Yours may be the most impenetrable shade that ever any but David or Adam have sat under, lamenting an Absalom or a Cain, cursed of God! But here is a ray from the throne; *'He knoweth the way that you take.'*

Job 23:13-14. 'But he is in one mind, and who can turn him? And what his soul desireth, even that he doeth. For he performeth the thing that is appointed for me: and many such things are with him.

> 1. It is the Lord's will that I should be thus tried by the fear that friend is for ever lost. 2 He will be glorified in this matter. 3. He chose this cross for me. 4. It is not a singular case; he sends many such 'heart-aches' and 'immedicable

wound', in order to give occasion to the display of his own matchless skill in healing.

2 Sam. 23:5. 'Although my house be not so with God [not as verse 4 describes], yet he hath made with me an everlasting covenant, ordered in all things sure'. Compare with this, David's most doleful and heart-rending lamentation over Absalom, in 2 Sam. 18:33. 'O my son Absalom', &c.

> You see to what David betook himself. He turned from dead and lost Absalom to the living *Jehovah,* whose grace and tender love shone so bright in the covenant.

Dan. 4:35. 'He doeth according to his will in the army of heaven, and among the inhabitants of the earth.'

Ezek. 14:22-23. 'Ye shall be comforted concerning the evil that I brought upon Jerusalem. And ye shall know that I have not done without cause all that I have done in it, saith the Lord.'

> There is fourfold comfort suggested here and in the context. 1. We shall see it was the Lord's will. 2. We shall have our thoughts drawn off the sad aspect of matters as they appear to us, and directed to the glory of God displayed therein. 3. We shall find a goodly company of saved ones, who sympathise with us and bring glory to God. 4. We shall see that, from beginning to end, there was a profound and most satisfactory reason for the whole providence of God in this matter.

Matt. 26:42. 'Thy will be done.'

1. Our Lord in the garden spoke thus, *q.d.* All that is needful toward the sinner's *justification,* let it come on me, however dark, however terrific, though it even for a time leave me cut off from thy manifested love. 2. Shall you not say in return, *q.d.* All that is needful toward my *sanctification,* let it come; even if it be the anguish of having to cry, 'Amen, Alleluia' (*Rev.* 19:2-3), in reference to friends overtaken and cut off in their sins.

Isa. 30:15. 'In returning and rest shall ye be saved; in quietness and confidence shall be your strength.'

Isa. 30:18. 'And therefore will the Lord wait that he may be gracious unto you, and therefore will he be exalted that he may have mercy upon you. For the Lord is a God of judgment [*i.e.* equity]. Blessed are all they that wait for him.'

Isa. 30:19. 'Thou shalt weep no more. He will be very gracious to thee at the voice of thy cry; when he shall hear it, he will answer thee.'

2 Cor. 4:17-18. 'For our light affliction, which is but for a moment, worketh for us a far more exceeding and eternal weight of glory, while we look not at the things which are seen.'

Look away—look up—look within the veil.[5]

---

[5] 'As he that is going through a strong running river is in danger to fall and drown by reason of the dizziness of his brain, unless he fix his eyes upon the bank, so shall we be ready to faint in affliction unless we look to the comfortable end thereof.'—*Bishop Cowper.*

Psa. 71:20. 'Thou, which hast shewed me great and sore troubles, shall quicken me again, and shalt bring me up again from the depths of the earth.'

> Though my stroke has laid me in a grave of anguish and gloom, thou wilt give me a resurrection; even as thou wilt do to my body after laying it in the tomb.[6]

Prov. 23:16. 'My son, give me thine heart.'

> Is not this the voice from thy friend's tomb? The Lord demands a surrender of your whole heart to *himself*. Put emphasis on 'ME', give thy heart to *me*, and to no other.

John 13:7. 'What I do thou knowest not now, but thou shalt know hereafter.'

> A sort of divine proverb.

Amos 5:8. 'Who turneth the shadow of death into the morning.'

> 'It is', says Bunyan, 'as ordinary as for the light to shine, for God to make black and dismal dispensations usher in bright and pleasing.'

Psa. 136:23. 'Who remembered us in our low estate: for his mercy endureth for ever.'

Isa. 40:27. 'Why sayest thou, O Jacob, and speakest, O Israel, My way is hid from the Lord, and my judgment

---

[6] 'God knoweth well how to use things, and will make us to be obliged to affliction, and to thank God who made us acquainted with such a rough companion to force us to Christ.'—*S. Rutherford.*

is passed over from my God!' Verse 23. 'Hast thou not known?'

> 'Your troubles issue from the same love that redeemed you from hell', says an old divine.

Isa. 28:24-25. 'Doth the plowman plow all day to sow? Doth he open and break the clods of his ground? When he hath made plain the face thereof, doth he not cast abroad the fitches, and scatter the cummin, and cast in the principal wheat, and the appointed barley, and the rye in their place?'

> God uses various methods with your soul to prepare it for various crops, like the skilful husbandman in preparing his field; and also, as set forth in verses 27-29, in thrashing out his harvest. Judson writes to a friend, *'Take the bitter cup with both hands,* and sit down to your repast. You will soon learn a secret that there is sweetness at the bottom! You will find it the sweetest cup you ever tasted all your life. You will find heaven coming near you.'

Introduction to Chapter 20

The Sorrowful—Widow and Orphan

The gospel when 'preached with the Holy Ghost sent down from heaven' (*1 Pet.* 1:12), has very different effects from that same gospel preached by us in our own strength. So is it with our attempts to carry the balm of Gilead to the wounds of sorrowing ones. We must have the Holy Spirit to apply all we say.

1. It is not out of place to remind even the widow and the orphan that all our affections tend to degenerate from God to human objects. We give friends too high a place, oftentimes. The wife, the mother, the husband, the father, the brother, sister, friend—insensibly entwine themselves round our soul so firmly that the oak-tree of love toward God is arrested in its growth. And it is the case of true believers that we are speaking of. It *may* have been so in the case of this person you visit. Dr Payson speaks of God's

kind wisdom acting in this case like the man who, finding a friend shutting himself up and idolising a set of lamps, rejoicing in their light, should begin by blowing out the lamps one by one; and who then, opening the shutters, lets in the light of the better sun.

2. We should show the *peculiar* interest which God takes in their case. This may be done by referring to such a passage as Proverbs 23:10-11, 'Enter not into the field of the fatherless; for their Redeemer is mighty, he will plead their cause with thee.' For here, *a.* we see the bereaved ones fixed on as special objects of God's attention. *b.* We see them represented as getting *the Lord* to step into the place of their natural protector. *c.* We hear a voice warning all men to beware of hurting a hair of their head. *d.* We hear that same voice speaking of them in a most tender, gracious, sympathising tone.

20

THE SORROWFUL—WIDOW AND ORPHAN

Psa. 23:1. 'The Lord is my shepherd, I shall not want.'

Psa. 23:6. 'Surely goodness and mercy shall follow me all the days of my life; and I shall dwell in the house of the Lord for ever.'

> If God is yours, sing this aloud, with your eye on the Saviour who is your peace. 1. As to this *present* life. Love that does you good, and love that pities you, shall never let you get beyond its reach. 2. As to the life *to come*. He that gave you his Son, will give you a home. 3. 'Surely' it shall be so; happen what may, be the amount of desolation what it may.

Isa. 55:19. 'The Lord shall be unto thee an everlasting light.'

Job 2:13. 'So they sat down with him upon the ground seven days and seven nights, and none spake a word unto him; for they saw his grief was very great.'

'It would be inhuman to deny the relief of mourning, when mourning itself is often its own relief.'—*Grosvenor*. 'Let sorrow have its way a while, and that will make way for comfort.'—*Caryl*. It is no new thing for the weary heart to desire rest beyond earth, Psa. 55:6.

Ruth 1:3, 5-6. 'And Elimelech, Naomi's husband, died, and she was left, and her two sons. And Mahlon and Chilion died also; and the woman was left of her two sons and her husband. Then she arose.'

> 1. The Lord records this widow's sorrows; for he took deep interest in them. 2. These bereavements turned her thoughts toward Israel's land again. 3. They ended in Ruth's conversion and blessing.

John 19:26-27. 'When Jesus therefore saw his mother, and the disciple standing by whom he loved, he saith unto his mother, Woman, behold thy son! Then he saith to the disciple, Behold thy mother!'

> 1. Jesus chooses the most loving to take charge of his bereaved mother, who was a widow, and who was now losing such a son! 2. Jesus did this at the moment when his woe was at its height.

Luke 7:13. 'And when the Lord saw her, he had compassion on her, and said unto her, Weep not.'

> Christ's pity for the widow's sorrows. 1. He meant to give her joy out of that bereavement. 2. So still, at this hour, he 'mindeth to distil heaven out of thy cross'.

John 11:33-35. 'When Jesus therefore saw her weeping, and the Jews also weeping which came with her, he groaned in the spirit and was troubled, and said, Where have ye laid him? They say unto him, Lord, come and see. Jesus wept.'

> 'He commandeth you to weep: and that princely One who took up to heaven with him a man's heart, to be a compassionate High Priest, became your fellow and companion on earth by weeping for the dead.' — *Samuel Rutherford.*

Psa. 103:14. 'He knoweth our frame.'

Psa. 103:13. 'Like as a father pitieth his children, so the Lord pitieth them that fear him.'

Jer. 49:11. 'Leave thy fatherless children; I will preserve them alive: and let thy widows trust in me.'

> While telling Edom that desolation should be such that their widows and orphans should have no other to trust in but the God of Israel whom they used to despise, he at the same time graciously encourages these bereaved ones. 1. Orphans, your fathers are gone! I offer myself as your guardian. 2. Widows, you have none to watch over you, 'trust in me'. 3. If he spoke thus to the families of his enemies, how much more to those of his own?

Exod. 22:22. 'Ye shall not afflict any widow, nor fatherless child.'[1]

Deut. 10:18. 'He doth execute the judgment of the

---

[1] 'Hath God charged others to take care of the fatherless and widows, and will he neglect them himself?' — *Sibbes.*

fatherless and widow, and loveth the stranger in giving him food and raiment.'

Psa. 146:9. 'He relieveth the fatherless and the widow.'

Psa. 10:14. 'Helper of the fatherless. The poor committeth himself to thee.'

Psa. 68:5. 'A father of the fatherless, and a judge of the widows, is God in his holy habitation.'

> '*Judge* of the widow' has a wide meaning, *viz.*, he who manages all her concerns and attends to all her interests. It is, *q.d.* He is to the widow and her family what Gideon, and Samson, and Samuel were to their nation.

Prov. 15:25. 'He will establish the border of the widows.'

> This is said in opposition to the 'house of the proud'. It implies, therefore, that the widow is one who, self-emptied, rests her soul on the Lord. 1. He saves her soul, giving her righteousness and the Spirit, out of Christ's stores. 2. He cares for her temporal interests, having given her the kingdom (*Luke* 12:32).

1 Tim. 5:5. 'She that is a widow indeed trusteth in God.'

> Bereft of other hopes, she clings to the undying One.

Hos. 14:3. 'In thee the fatherless findeth mercy.'

> 1. One that ceases from all that is human help, and has only God to resort to, is welcome to him. 2. So also one that is compelled to leave human objects of confidence, because they are stricken by death, is welcome to the Lord instead.

Isa. 54:5. 'Thy Maker is thy husband.'

> Spoken primarily to Israel, long, long desolate. It may be
> applied to you recently made desolate. 'Thy Maker', *i.e.*
> he who maketh thee his own by redemption, as he made
> thee his creature by creation, this same Jehovah presents
> himself to thee as 'thy Husband', to show thee kindness,
> care, love, and fellowship.

Jer. 17:7-8. 'Blessed is the man that trusteth in the Lord,
. . . he shall not be careful in the year of drought, neither
shall cease from yielding fruit.'[2]

James 1:27. 'Pure religion and undefiled before God
and the Father is this, To visit the fatherless and widows
in their affliction.'

> 1. The word *'religion'* means the outward profession made,
> or the outward ceremonial of religious profession. 2. So
> pitiful is our God to the bereaved, that he says to all his
> people, 'Show the faith that is in your heart by imitating, in
> outward acts of kindness to orphans and widows, the love
> of your Master.' 3. This care of the widow and orphan is
> most acceptable to our God, who has a 'Father's' heart.

2 Cor. 1:3-4. 'Blessed be God, the Father of our Lord
Jesus Christ, the Father of mercies and the God of all
comfort, who comforteth us in all our tribulation, that
we may be able to comfort them which are in any trouble,

---

[2] Mr Shaw desired to have it recorded, that when he had buried with
his own hands, in the time of the plague, two of his family, God was
all-sufficient.

by the comfort wherewith we ourselves are comforted of God.'[3]

2 Cor. 7:6. 'God that comforteth those that are cast down.'

Psa. 27:10. 'When my father and my mother forsake [leave] me, then the Lord will take me up.'[4]

> Implying evidently that the Lord will—1. Be able to do all a father or a mother ever did. 2. Be willing also so to do. As it is written of him in the verses that we next give.

Isa. 64:13. 'As one whom his mother comforteth, so will I comfort you.'

Isa. 9:6. 'The everlasting Father.'

Jer. 31:9. 'I am a Father to Israel.'

Nah. 1:7. 'The Lord is good; a stronghold in the day of trouble; and he knoweth them that trust in him.'

1 Cor. 3:21. 'Let no man glory in men; for all things are yours.'

> You can do without men—without father, mother, child. For 'all things are yours', because 'ye are Christ's.' It is recorded in the *Scots Worthies,* that a dying son wiped off his mother's tears, saying, 'Mother, you will find me in the *all-sufficiency of God.'*

---

[3] 'If man could find no comfort, and yet set himself to teach and encourage weak Christians, he frequently, by way of reflection, would receive great comfort himself.'—*Sibbes.*

[4] The principle is the same when other relatives are removed. A mother who lost two sons in one day said, 'I see God will leave me nothing to love but himself.'—*R. Venning.*

Deut. 8:3. 'Man doth not live by bread only, but by every word that proceedeth from out of the mouth of the Lord doth man live.' Compare Matthew 4:4.

> That is, by whatever God commands, or directs to happen, or bids be sent to thee.

Gen. 35:18. 'She called his name Benoni [son of my sorrow]; but his father called him Benjamin [right hand son].'

> There is a dark and a bright side to every such providence, as there was to the guiding pillar-cloud. *Nature* fixes on the dark and calls it 'sorrow';[5] faith sees the sun dispersing the darkness, and calls it by the name of joy.

Prov. 14:10. 'The heart knoweth its own bitterness.'

> And so also the Lord Jesus knows it. And what is more, he knows, by his own past experience of sorrow, how to turn 'Marah' into 'Elim'.

Isa. 32:2. 'A man shall be as an hiding-place.'

> 1. If friends weary of you and of your complaints and sorrows, remember that Jesus not only gives a shelter, but is himself a shelter. 2. One of the forms in which he becomes so to you is this, letting you tell him all you feel.

John 16:33. 'These things have I spoken unto you, that in me ye might have peace. In the world ye shall have tribulation.'

---

[5] Hence one expostulated thus, 'You will not meet God in the sanctuary because such a one is dead! That is, you will have nothing to do with God at a time when you need him so much.'

The springs of consolation are, like the snows of Lebanon, so high that they never are dried up. 1. What Christ has spoken should give us peace; *viz.*—what he has told us of his salvation, and the love shown to us therein. 2. These things are applied by the Comforter (verses 14-15). 3. These things are applied in times of trouble like the present.

Isa. 38:15. 'Himself hath done it.'

'Himself hath done it.' He who has searched me through
    Sees how I cleave to earth's ensnaring ties;
And so he breaks each reed on which my soul
    Too much for happiness and joy relies.

'Himself hath done it.' He would have me see
    What broken cistern human friends must prove,
That I may turn and quench my burning thirst
    At His own fount of ever-living love.

Introduction to Chapter 21

Sorrowful because of Forebodings and Cares

Our errand being one of grace, the Lord will hear us when we ask his presence in it. Now, his Spirit is not 'the spirit of fear': it is the 'spirit of love, and of power, and of a sound mind' (2 *Tim.* 1:7). To be clothed with his Spirit ourselves, and to ask him to impart to others what we ourselves are furnished with, is our best preparation for dealing with the case before us.

We may take up some such passage as Gen. 21:17, 'What aileth thee, Hagar?' Here is, *a.* God's interest in the cares and troubles of a servant-woman, or rather slave, *b.* God takes so deep an interest in such a case even as hers, that he sends an angel—ay, and no common angel; he sends 'the Angel of the Covenant', as appears by the context. *c.* The Holy Ghost has recorded all this minutely, to teach us what to expect when we too are in a wilderness, losing our way, and trying to manage our own cares.

Or we dwell upon Psa. 112:4, 'Unto the upright there ariseth light in the darkness.' A memorable text. *a.* As surely as there is a blue sky behind these dark clouds, so surely there is a gracious God and Father, though unseen, behind these distressing cares. *b.* The past has given examples of light arising in darkness. *c.* Your one duty is, to continue conscientiously and filially to attend to his will, doing or suffering.

Perhaps we may occasionally, with advantage, advert to history or biography. What a simple yet powerfully instructive incident was that of the little child, who, seeing her mother's tears while gazing shoreward from the ship that bore her amid strangers to a land of strangers, repeated (as she touched her mother's hand), 'Though I take the wings of the morning, and dwell in the uttermost parts of the sea, even there shall thy hand lead me, and thy right hand shall hold me'; and then asked, 'Is it true?'

21

SORROWFUL BECAUSE OF
FOREBODINGS AND CARES

1 Cor. 10:13. 'There hath no temptation [or, *trial,* in the widest sense] taken you but what is common to man: but God is faithful, who will not suffer you to be tempted [or, *tried* in any way] beyond what you are able; but will with the temptation [or, *trial,* whether it be small or great] also make a way to escape, that ye may be able to bear it.'

Gen. 21:17. 'What aileth thee, Hagar? Fear not; for God hath heard the voice of the lad where he is.'

Psa. 112:4. 'Unto the upright there ariseth light in the darkness.'

Psa. 37:23. 'The steps of a good man are ordered by the Lord, and he delighteth in his way.'

1. The plan of that man's life has been drawn up by the Lord, and he delights to see the plan carried out, step by step.
2. Each man's history is a world's history in miniature.

Num. 14:11. 'How long will this people provoke me? How long will it be ere they believe me, for all the signs that I have shewed among them?'

> What! not trust him with the future? He that has destroyed Pharaoh, is he not able to bring Anakims down? He that gave you his Spirit to bring you to know his Son (having given you his Son as your Saviour), what else will he hesitate to do for you?

Luke 12:29-32. 'Seek not ye what ye shall eat or what ye shall drink, neither be ye of doubtful mind. For all these things do the nations of the world seek after. And your Father knoweth that ye have need of these things. But rather seek ye the kingdom of God, and all these things shall be added unto you. Fear not, little flock; for it is your Father's good pleasure to give you the kingdom.'

> 1. He that has loved you, and who so loves you as to have ready for you the glorious kingdom, cannot but intend to keep you safe by the way. 2. But strength is not promised to be furnished *today* for the trials of *tomorrow*.

Matt. 10:30. 'The very hairs of your head are all numbered.'

1 Sam. 2:9. 'He will keep the feet of his saints.'

Rom. 8:28. 'We know that all things work together for good to them that love God, to them who are the called according to his purpose.'

> 1. 'All things?' yes, cares and perplexities, as well as other

things. 2. They will help on your progress. 3. They are in God's plan of your life—'according to his purpose'. 4. Do not say, 'If I were an eminent saint I might fancy this to be so'; for it belongs to all who *'love God', i.e.* who acquiesce in his will, who love the work and person of his Son, in whom the Father is revealed. 5. *'We know'* all this; we *'know'* it—it is most sure.

Prov. 12:21. 'There shall no evil happen to the just.'[1]

1. The just man in God's sight is the *sinner made just,* or justified,—the sinner 'in Christ, who walketh not after the flesh, but after the Spirit' (*Rom.* 8:1). 2. To this man, nothing but good ever comes. No condemnation, no wrath, no evil. 3. Trials and uncertainties drive him nearer to God, and so become blessings.

Psa. 112:7. 'He shall not be afraid of evil tidings: his heart is fixed, trusting on the Lord.'

The Good News takes the sting out of all that men call *evil tidings.* God's covenant love sweetens the bitterest gall.

Psa. 61:2. 'From the end of the earth will I cry unto thee, when my heart is overwhelmed: lead me to the rock that is higher than I.'

The Rock can cast its shadow over the careful, fearful, foreboding man, as it did over that same man when sin-oppressed, ready to sink under God's crushing wrath.

[1] 'If we are not secure from trials, we are secure from harm.'—*Cecil.* In the *Diary of Ruth Bryan,* the Editor has this notice, 'Observe the sweets of either mental care, or bodily affliction, when the Lord condescendingly and sovereignly moistens it and mellows it, by his sweet presence and blessed power.'

Phil. 4:6-7. 'Be careful for nothing, but in everything, by prayer and supplication with thanksgiving, let your requests be made known unto God; and the peace of God, which passeth all understanding, shall keep your hearts and minds through Christ Jesus.'[2]

Gen. 22: 8, 14. 'And Abraham said, My son, God will provide himself a lamb for a burnt-offering. So they went both of them together . . . And Abraham called the name of that place Jehovah-Jireh, as it is said to this day, In the mount of the Lord it shall be seen.'

'Jehovah-Jireh', The Lord will provide, or see to it.[3]

2 Cor. 1:9. '. . . we should not trust in ourselves, but in God who raiseth the dead.'

> *It is the Lord, whose mighty skill*
> *Can from afflictions raise*
> *Matter to fill eternity*
> *With everlasting praise.*

Rev. 2:10. 'Fear none of those things which thou shalt suffer.'

---

[2] Luther called prayer, 'The leeches of his care.' And another has said, 'In the very act of making known everything to God, his peace fills our souls.'

[3] 'Mrs C. is a miracle of patience. Though she has a confirmed cancer on each breast, she appears quite cheerful, and sings, walking about the house as if nothing was the matter, notwithstanding she has witnessed the suffering and death of her sister of the same disease. She leaves the matter with God. *N.B.*—Mrs C. lived only a few years after this, and then, before the disease had been developed, died suddenly. How wise to commit her course to him who cared for her.'—*Life of Mrs Hawkes.*

1 Cor. 10:2. 'They drank of the Rock that followed them.'

> God in the Pillar-Cloud, often called the Rock of salvation, was their spiritual drink, and was ever with them.

Matt. 13:22. 'The care of this world and the deceitfulness of riches choke the word.' Compare 1 Cor. 7:32. 'I would have you without carefulness.'

1 Pet. 5:7. 'Casting all your care upon him; for he careth for you.'

> 1. It is not, 'Cast *away* care', but 'Cast it *on Christ.*' 2. It is cast it *all* on him. 3. Not one concern of yours is too small for him. In creation, the smallest insect is cared for, and gets mysterious life, as certainly as the loftiest angel; and in providence, his saints' minutest interest is attended to. 'If it were not so, I would have told you' (*John 14:2*). 4. Let this sink into your heart '*He* careth for *you.*'

Jer. 17:7-8. 'Blessed is the man that trusteth in the Lord . . . he shall not be careful in the year of drought.'

> *Faith* is the remedy for *fear* and *care*.

Mark 4:39-40. 'The wind ceased, and there was a great calm; and he said unto them, Why are ye so fearful? How is it that ye have no faith?'

> 1. You will see, when the storm is over, how unreasonable was your fear. 2. He that permits the storm to arise can control it. 3. Fix your eye on him; forget the winds and waves.

Jer. 10:23. 'O Lord, I know that the way of man is not in himself. It is not in him that walketh to direct his steps.'[4]

Psa. 31:15. 'My times are in thy hand.'

Psa. 32:1, 8. 'Blessed is he whose transgression is forgiven, whose sin is covered, . . . I will instruct thee and teach thee the way which thou shalt go: I will guide thee with mine eye.'

> 1. A pardoned man is one to whom guidance is promised. Why then should he be so careful, and fearful? 2. He that sees how to get over the difficulties in the way of thy pardon, can he not get over the difficulties that lie in thy way through life?

Num. 9:2, 18-22. 'Let the children of Israel also keep the passover at his appointed season . . . At the commandment of the Lord, the children of Israel journeyed, and at the commandment of the Lord they pitched. Whether it were two days, or a week, or a year, that the cloud tarried upon the tabernacle, remaining thereon, the children of Israel abode in their tents and journeyed not; but when it was taken up, they journeyed.'

> 1. Passover-men are the men whom the Lord will guide by his cloudy pillar. This is the connecting link between the first part of this chapter and the second. 2. They are not left to shift for themselves. 3. He often takes unexpected

---

[4] 'If so you need not wish to alter anything. God has chosen for you out of his endless stores the very best portion',—says one who knew care.

paths, and puts them to much inconvenience. 4. He thus trains their will.

Isa. 42:16. 'I will bring the blind by a way that they knew not; I will lead them in paths that they have not known. I will make darkness light before them, and crooked things straight. These things will I do unto them, and not forsake them.'[5]

Gen. 46:2-3. 'God spake unto Israel in the visions of the night, and said, Jacob, Jacob? And he said, Here am I. And he said, I am God! the God of thy father! Fear not to go down into Egypt.' Verse 4. 'I will go down with thee into Egypt.'

Psa. 94:18-19. 'Thy mercy, O Lord, held me up. In the multitude of my thoughts within me, thy comforts delight my soul.'

> 1. '*Mercy* held him up' when his foot was slipping. *Mercy! mercy!* the very thing for my case. 2. God's comforts were dropped into the stream of his anxious thoughts. Yes, *the comforts of God!*

Isa. 50:10. 'Who is among you that feareth the Lord, that obeyeth the voice of his servant, that walketh in darkness and hath no light? Let him trust in the name of the Lord, and stay upon his God.'

---

[5] 'I am learning to read love in the greatest of evils, desertions, afflictions, plagues of the heart. And when anything comes, though never so cross, I first inquire, 'What love can I see in this?'—*Nisbet's Tracts.*

1. Spoken to a real believer, *i.e.* to a sinner who is a 'fearer of Jehovah', that is, who feels the Lord's majesty, and at the same time the grace revealed by Messiah, 'his servant'. 2. Spoken to such a one specially in times of affliction, for the *darkness* here is that arising from outward things, which the afflicted is apt to regard as equivalent to God's frowns. 3. Let such a one fix his thoughts on 'the *name* of the Lord', *i.e.* the Lord's manifested character, including the Lord's gracious heart, and stay himself thereon, till 'these calamities be overpast'.

Gen. 32:7, 9, 11, 30. 'Then Jacob was greatly afraid and distressed. And Jacob said, O God of my father Abraham . . . deliver me! And Jacob called the name of the place *Peniel,* for I have seen God face to face, and my life is preserved.'

> 1. It was always in anxious seasons that Jacob got his singular discoveries of God. This is one instance; but see also, Bethel, ch. 28:11-12, and Bethel again, ch. 35:5, 9, and 46:3-4. How seasonable is our God's support. 2. If so, perplexities and forebodings may be but the folding-doors at which we are to see God come forth (as Jonathan came out to David from the thick wood) to comfort us.

Song of Sol. 4:8. 'Come with me from Lebanon, my spouse, with me from Lebanon; look from the top of Amana, from the top of Shenir and Hermon, from the lions' dens, from the mountains of the leopards.'

1 Pet. 5:10-11. 'But the God of all grace, who hath called us to his eternal glory by Christ Jesus, after that ye have suffered a while, make you perfect, stablish, strengthen, settle you. To him be glory and dominion for ever and ever Amen.'

1. It is the God of grace, that wishes us to suffer a while, the God who has spared us every drop of penal suffering. 2. If so, these trials must be love-potions. 3. They will soon end. 4. They will contribute to our after completeness. The potter is handling and moulding the clay at present, and sometimes his hand seems rude as it shapes the vessel. 5. We shall yet sing 'Glory' to him over these very sorrows; and 'Dominion', too, rejoicing that he had the power to overrule.

2 Chron. 20:12. 'Neither know we what to do; but our eyes are upon thee.'

It is he that drives the chariot, he alone. Do not try to help him, but sit quiet, resting in faith upon him, and look at what he will do. 'The Lord, alone, did lead him' (*Deut.* 32:12).

Psa. 25:15. 'Mine eyes are ever toward the Lord for he shall pluck my feet out of the net.'

Job 9:34. 'Let him take his rod away from me.'

'It is all one to have a burden taken off, and to have strength given to bear and patience to endure it.' — *Caryl*.

Psa. 56:3. 'What time I am afraid, I will trust in thee.'

Dan. 3:17. 'If it be so, our God whom we serve is able to deliver us from the burning fiery furnace.'

Isa. 27:8. 'He stayeth his rough wind in the day of his east wind.'

> He might have added to this trial bodily sickness or the sickness of friends; he might have added excruciating pain; he might have added a hundred aggravations; but lo! he gives you just so much at a time as, through his Spirit in you, you may be able to bear.

1 John 4:4. 'Greater is he that is in you, than he that is in the world.'

Isa. 27:7. 'Hath he smitten him as he smote those that smote him?'

> There is a wide difference between your afflictions and those of other men, if you are one of his people—even as there was between Israel's chastisement and Pharaoh's doom.

Psa. 140:7. 'O Lord God, the strength of my salvation! thou hast covered my head in the day of battle.'

Psa. 42:7. 'All thy waves and billows are gone over me.'

> It is *God's waves*. 'Tides of love springing out of the ocean of God's love! so that they cannot overwhelm,—but only plunge us in its unfathomable depths.'—(*A. Newton's Mem.*)

Luke 10:19. 'Nothing shall by any means hurt you.'

> Spoken to the seventy—to all whose names are written in heaven. Jesus promises, 1. *Nothing* shall hurt a disciple!

2. Nothing shall hurt a disciple, come in what shape it may, and though Satan try to wield it—'Nothing by *any means!*'

Introduction to Chapter 22

Sorrowful because of Worldly Circumstances

Oh to be ourselves furnished with the 'Spirit of meekness and temperance' (*Gal.* 5:23), in going to those who mourn because of worldly circumstances. The Holy Ghost gives *'meekness'*, *i.e.* acquiescence in God's will, the sinking of our will into his; and he gives also *'temperance'*, *i.e.* that state of mind in which we sit loose to the world—not too much affected by either its joys or sorrows, its riches or poverty, its meat or drink, its business or pleasure, its health or sickness, its prosperity or adversity.

1. Sympathy, expressed in our very tone, and coming from the heart, must preface, or rather be mingled with, our attempts to use such circumstances advantageously. This is itself the most penetrating of all consolation, for it

is as Bacon (quoted by Buchanan *on Affliction*) says, 'The law of sympathy seems to be, that it redoubleth joys and cutteth griefs in halves. No man that imparteth his joys to his friends but joyeth more; so no man that imparteth his griefs, to his friends but he grieveth less.'

2. From broken cisterns let us point to the fountain of living waters. Suppose we take Exod. 3:7, 'I know their sorrows.' *a.* We tell of the Lord's heart of compassion, how it yearns over sorrowing ones in any adversity. *b.* We tell how it yearns to bring the sorrowing to bathe their weary soul in the joy that is beyond all other joy, the joy of acceptance, pardon, favour. *c.* We speak of the kindness of the Lord, in not withering the gourd without at the same time pointing you to the shadow of the Great Rock. *d.* We suggest the probability of his providence interposing ere long even as to temporal matters, 'For your heavenly Father knoweth that you have need of all these things' (*Matt.* 6:32).

22

SORROWFUL BECAUSE OF
WORLDLY CIRCUMSTANCES

Eccles. 7:13. 'Consider the work of God; for who can make that straight which he hath made crooked.'

> 1. 'Whatever crook there is in a man's lot it is of God's making; and every man has some crook.'[1] 2. But the thought that it is God's doing contains in it an unspeakable amount of comfort. 'God's wisdom made choice of it for me' said one, 'and it must be the best, because it was his choice.'[2]

Joel 2:13-14. 'Turn to the Lord your God. Who knoweth if he will return and repent, and leave a blessing behind him?' And verse 25, 'I will restore to you the years that the locust hath eaten, the canker-worm, and the caterpillar, and the pelmer-worm; my great army which I sent among you.'

> 1. The Lord can in a day make up years of grief and

[1] See Boston's *Crook in the Lot*.
[2] 'It is a ground of comfort to God's people, that while they are suffering, his will is doing.' — *Caryl*.

adversity. 2. Remember how he turned Job's captivity. 3. Meanwhile turn to himself. He who both gave your temporal mercies, and withdrew them, gave you long ago his own beloved Son and has not withdrawn that best of gifts.

Exod. 3:7. 'I know their sorrows.'

1 Chron. 4:9-10. 'And Jabez was more honourable than his brethren; and his mother called his name Jabez ['sorrowful one'], saying, Because I bare him with sorrow. And Jabez called on the God of Israel, saying, Oh that thou wouldest bless me indeed, and enlarge my coast, and that thine hand might be with me, and that thou wouldest keep me from evil that it may not grieve me! And God granted him that which he requested.'

> 1. Here the most honourable in God's sight is found in deep affliction. 2. His worldly circumstances had to do with this sorrowful prayer. 3. He sought help from the God in whom his soul rested. 4. He sought blessing on the exertions he meant to make. 5. He prayed to be kept from evil, as much as to have his coast enlarged.

Job 1:21. 'The Lord gave, and the Lord hath taken away.'[3]

> 1. Remember this man's immense losses. 2. Listen to his calm acquiescence in God's dealing. 3. His impatience was but of a day's continuance, and was an exception to his behaviour on every other occasion.

[3] 'What is the use of murmurs? You cannot sin yourself out of your troubles.'—*Brooks.* Another says, 'God parts that and us which would part us and him.'—*R. Venning.*

Job 42:12. 'So the Lord blessed the latter end of Job more than his beginning.'

> 1. Remember how he took his losses (1:21). Then 2. Remember his consolation under them, *e.g.* (19:25), 'I know that my Redeemer liveth.' 3. See here the issue, even in this life.

Psa. 69:16. 'Hear me, O Lord, for thy loving-kindness is good.'

Psa. 42:7-8. 'Deep calleth unto deep at the noise of thy waterspouts; all thy waves and thy billows are gone over me. Yet the Lord will command his loving-kindness in the daytime, and in the night his song shall be with me, and my prayer [shall be] unto the God of my life.'

Psa. 30:5. 'Weeping may endure for a night, but joy cometh in the morning.'

Deut. 8:3. 'And he humbled thee, and suffered thee to hunger and fed thee with manna, which thou knewest not, neither did thy fathers know, that he might make thee know that man doth not live by bread alone; but by every word that proceedeth out of the mouth of the Lord doth man live.'

> By whatever God chooses to command, man lives.

Phil. 4:11-12. 'I have learned, in whatever state I am, therewith to be content. I know both how to be abased, and I know how to abound; everywhere and in all things

I am instructed both to be full and to be hungry, both to abound and to suffer need.'

> This lesson is one learned by much teaching. In verse 13 the secret of it appears, *'through Christ strengthening me'*.

Hab. 3:17-18. 'Although the fig-tree shall not blossom . . . yet will I be glad in the Lord.'

Joel 3:16. 'The heavens and the earth shall shake; but the Lord will be the hope of his people, and the strength of the children of Israel.'[4]

1 Sam. 30:3, 6. 'So David and his men came to the city, and behold it was burnt with fire, and their wives, and their sons, and their daughters, were taken captives. And David was greatly distressed; for the people spake of stoning him . . . But David encouraged himself in the Lord his God.'

> 1. An accumulation of disasters here! All his own property, and all his own family away! His people's property, and his people's families away! And then his people blame him for the loss of all! And they threaten his life! though up to this moment they would have given their own lives for his at any time. 2. Under this accumulation of distresses, he has one comfort, and it is enough 'HIS GOD'. The God who has redeemed us from our sins, what can he not save us from?

Psa. 37:3-4. 'Trust in the Lord, and do good, so shalt

---

[4] 'The Lord can make the death of these comforts as the scythe to the meadow.'—*Brooks*.

thou dwell in the land, and verily thou shalt be fed. Delight thyself also in the Lord, and he shall give thee the desire of thine heart.'[5]

Psa. 138:7. 'Though I walk in the midst of trouble, thou wilt revive me. Thou shalt stretch forth thine hand against the wrath of mine enemies, and thy right hand shall save me.'

Psa. 55:22. 'Cast thy burden upon the Lord, and he shall sustain thee.'

> Remember; either, he will remove the load; or he will increase your strength to bear it.

Rom. 8:18-19. 'I reckon that the sufferings of this present time are not worthy to be compared with the glory which shall be revealed in us. For the earnest expectation of the creature waiteth for the manifestation of the sons of God.'

> The hope of that coming day of deliverance should cheer us now. It is a day for which 'the creature', *i.e.* creation at large, waits. In that day God's children shall be openly manifested to be such; their reproach wiped away, their poverty removed, their resurrection robes put on.

Heb. 10:33. '. . . Ye took joyfully the spoiling of your goods, knowing in yourselves that ye have in heaven a

---

[5] 'There is a mystery (and depth in the mystery) not only of election and reprobation, but of God's providence. No reason can be given why some of God's children are quiet, and others greatly afflicted, why one should be poor and another rich.'—*Sibbes' Medit.*

better and an enduring substance.'

> What cheered the martyr-sufferers should cheer you. And remember, as it is truly said, 'The pain of pain is impatience under it' (*Adams*), so is it with losses.

Rev. 13:10. 'Here is the patience and the faith of the saints.' And 14:12. 'Here is the patience of the saints: here are they that keep the commandments of God, and the faith of Jesus.'[6]

> It is in trying circumstances that faith is best seen; and that patience arising from faith is best manifested. Your trials are a platform on which God designs to exhibit to the world how he can enable his own to endure.

Gen. 18:14. 'Is anything too hard for the Lord?'

> 'No cause is so desperate, but God may right it.' — *Boston.*

---

[6] 'Many speak as if the whole of religion consisted in *activity*, whereas the *patience* of the saints is equally honouring to God.' And Brooks says, 'Mercy is nearest when a person sits silent under the greatest troubles.'

Introduction to Chapter 23

Sorrowful because of Persecution, Lack of Sympathy, or the Like

'If ye be reproached for the name of Christ, happy are ye; for the Spirit of glory and of God resteth upon you.' (*1 Pet.* 4:14). Let us go forth, praying that that Spirit may use our visit to refresh his weary ones, 'seeing he delighteth in them'.

1. We aim at the honour of conveying the Master's sympathy to such sorrowful ones. In seeking this end, perhaps we remind them how the whole word of God is strewed over with passages directed to cases like theirs. All past generations of the Lord's people have felt somewhat as they; all have been sufferers. And, knowing it was to be so, the Lord stored his Word with thoughts for them under their peculiar trials.

2. We try to find some special token of the Lord's kind-

ness in the midst of this afflictive dealing. Are they reduced to inactivity, and forbid to labour? We remind them that it was said to David, 'It was well that the thought was in thine heart.' Are they deprived of ordinances and privileges? Remind them of the saying, 'Man shall not live by bread alone' (*Deut.* 8:3). 'She that tarried at home divided the spoil' (*Psa.* 68:12). 'As his part is that goeth down to the battle, so shall his part be that tarrieth by the stuff; they shall part alike. And it was so from that day forward, that he made it a statute and an ordinance for Israel, unto this day' (*1 Sam.* 30:24-25).

3. We turn with them to the never-failing, ever fresh, ever cool streams from Lebanon—we set forth the person, as well as the work, of Jesus. We speak of him in his living sympathies, and in the strength of his arm. We try to leave the sorrowful at his feet, or leaning on his breast, using his blood to bathe their sinful souls therewith, and using all that is in him to supply the lack of all taken from, or denied to, them.

23

SORROWFUL BECAUSE OF PERSECUTION, LACK OF SYMPATHY, OR THE LIKE

Acts 14:22. '. . . exhorting them to continue in the faith, and that we must through much tribulation enter into the kingdom of God.'

> You are on the path traversed by the believers of Lystra, Iconium, and Antioch. Barnabas travelled by this road. Paul was seldom on any other. So the Thessalonians, too. 1 Thess. 3:3-4.

Matt. 5:11-12. 'Blessed are ye when men shall revile you, and persecute you, and shall say all manner of evil against you falsely, for my sake. Rejoice ye, and be exceeding glad; for great is your reward in heaven: for so persecuted they the prophets that were before you.'[1]

---

[1] 'The scullion scours the silver vessel, and makes it clear and bright for the Master's use.'—*Caryl*. 'Losses, crosses, disappointments, ill tongues, loss of friends, relatives, houses, or country, are God's workmen, set to work out good to you out of everything that befalleth you.'—*S. Rutherford*.

Neh. 2:19-20. '. . . They laughed us to scorn, and despised us, and said, What is this thing that ye do? Will ye rebel against the king? Then answered I them, and said unto them, The God of heaven, he will prosper us; therefore we his servants will arise and build.'

> Here is the eye of the saints lifted upward to the Lord, when enemies hoped that the sight of their array would daunt and subdue the courage of the strongest of them.

Psa. 119:141. 'I am small and despised; yet do I not forget thy precepts.'

> 1. Others have been as unsympathised with as you. 2. The Lord's precepts were found sufficient even then. The words evidently signify, 'When I feel myself thus overlooked and forgotten, I turn to your revelation and find fellowship with you.'

John 8:29. 'And he that sent me is with me: the Father hath not left me alone.'

John 16:32. 'Ye shall be scattered, every man to his own, and shall leave me alone; and yet I am not alone, because the Father is with me.'

> Job (6:15-20) found that his friends were like brooks, which dry up in summer by reason of the heat. So also did Jesus. But even in the heat of the fierceness of wrath, Jesus found the Father's presence to be his water-brooks. He has left us an example; and the *Comforter* takes these things and shows them to us, adding, 'This same Jesus has, in his human heart, a well of sympathy for forsaken

ones, even because, when on earth, lover and friend stood aloof from his sore.'

Psa. 116:11-12. 'I said in my haste [hasting like a passoverman out of Egypt], All men are liars. What shall I render unto the Lord for all his benefits toward me?'

Psa. 142:4-5. 'I looked on my right hand, and beheld, but there was no man that would know me: refuge failed me; no man cared for my soul! I cried unto thee, O Lord: I said, Thou art my refuge, my portion in the land of the living.'

> 1. Christ, the Head of the Church, so felt on earth, and so speaks of what he felt. 2. Every member, therefore, of the Church, who feels thus desolate, may be sure to find in him the fullest sympathy, as well as guidance.

Heb. 4:15. 'We have not an high priest that cannot be touched with the feeling of our infirmities.

> 1. *'Infirmities'*, i.e. our want of ability to do and bear; our need of help and strength. 2. We have one who, far from being incapable of sympathy, is easily touched by our case. 'There is' (says one) 'human sympathy as well as divine in the bosom of him who on earth appropriated to himself all our sins, sorrows, and deaths and who is now seated on the throne of heavenly power to deliver us from them all.' 3. So then Jesus is not like Caiaphas, nor even as old Eli (*1 Sam.* 1:14), but is tender, and loving, and wise.

Rom. 8:26. 'Likewise the Spirit also helpeth our infirmities.'

Isa. 30:18. 'The Lord is a God of judgment; blessed are all they that wait for him.'

Acts 9:4. 'Saul, Saul, why persecutest thou me?' Compared with Zech. 2:8. 'He that toucheth you, toucheth the apple of his eye.'

> Here is the *head* and the *members* identified in feeling—the head looking down to see what thorn has pierced the foot, or who has struck the hand. 2. You may pray, as Psa. 17:8, 'Keep me as the apple of the eye!'

Dan. 11:35. 'And some of them of understanding shall fall, to try them, and to purge and make them white, even to the end of time.'

> Compare Dan. 12:10. 'Many shall be purified, made white, and tried.' The trials have wrought well. The tried ones are blessed thereby, none lost.

Rev. 7:4, 14:1. 'I heard the number of them which were sealed; and there were sealed an hundred forty and four thousand of all the tribes of Israel!' 'And I looked, and, lo! a Lamb stood on Mount Sion, and with him an hundred forty and four thousand, having his Father's name written on their foreheads.'

> 1. These were sealed as God's servants and then exposed to furious storms. 2. Yet *not one* is lost. There were 144,000 sealed; there are 144,000 on Sion. 3. They are perfected in holiness, 'having his Father's name.'

1 Pet. 3:14. 'But if ye suffer for righteousness' sake, happy are ye.'

James 5:7-8. 'Be patient, therefore, brethren, until the coming of the Lord . . . Be ye also patient, for the coming of the Lord draweth nigh.'

> He tells them of fruit sure to result from opposition and trial. He tells also that it is chiefly at Christ's coming again that this fruit is to be reaped. But it is worth waiting for. 'Behold the husbandman.'[2]

Psa. 37:1. 'Fret not thyself because of evil-doers.'

> 'Murmuring', says Brooks, 'is a time-destroying sin. The murmurer is the hieroglyphic of folly.' And another says: 'The wicked may hold the bitter cup to your head, but God mixes it, and there is no poison in it.'

Zech. 1:11-13. '. . . behold, all the earth sitteth still, and is at rest. Then the Angel of the Lord answered and said, O Lord of Hosts, how long wilt thou not have mercy on Jerusalem, and on the cities of Judah, against which thou hast had indignation these threescore and ten years? And the Lord answered the Angel that talked with me with good words and comfortable words.'

> 1. Earth may take no interest in God's Israel, but God does. 2. Christ, the Angel of his presence, forgets not to take up their case. 3. How he pleads! 4. What an overflow of love in the Father's reply!

[2] 'Glory follows afflictions, not as the day follows night, but as spring follows winter. Winter prepares the earth for spring; so do afflictions sanctified prepare the soul for glory.'—*Sibbes*.

2 Thess. 2:16-17. 'Now our Lord Jesus Christ himself, and God even our Father, which hath loved us, and given us everlasting consolation and good hope through grace, comfort your hearts, and establish you in every good word and work.'

Job 12:4. 'I am as one mocked of his neighbour, who calleth on God, and he answereth him.'[3]

Isa. 26:20. 'Come, my people, enter thou into thy chambers, and shut thy doors about thee; hide thyself as it were for a little moment, until the indignation be overpast.'

Hag. 2:5. 'My Spirit remaineth among you; fear ye not.'

Isa. 41:17. 'When the poor and needy seek water, and there is none, and their tongue faileth for thirst, I the Lord will hear them, I the God of Israel will not forsake them.'

[3] 'Will you not be thankful for this, *viz.*, that he should take such pains to teach you that he alone is worthy of your love.'—*Nisbet's Tracts.*

Introduction to Chapter 24

The Sorrow of the World

'The fruit of the Spirit is love, joy, peace' (*Gal*. 5:22). It is he that can produce the very opposite state of mind from that with which we have here to deal. 'O send forth thy light and thy truth! Let them lead me!'

1. This state of mind, 'sorrow of the world', when found in any degree in real believers, must be most carefully dealt with. It is too often found in some measure in Christian souls, and in any case is it sure to scorch the soul. Indeed, for the time, it makes the soul a Gilboa 'on which falls no dew'. *a*. In meeting such cases among believers, use kindness and sympathy; then remind them that now is their time to exhibit what the Lord can do for them in absence of all earthly joy. Dwell on this; seek to stir their souls by this thought. *b*. Set before them, as for the first time, what there is in the Lord Jesus Christ for empty souls. Satan

and the world and corruption are clouds darkening the sky; therefore, set the *sun* before them by repeated statements regarding the wise and holy sovereignty of God, and regarding Christ in his work, Christ in his person, Christ in his holy love. *c.* Use some passage of the Word. *d.* Tell the danger of giving way to this morbid state. You may perhaps be able to point to well-known instances of the evil, such as that published some years ago as a beacon—the case of a minister of the gospel. He was zealous and faithful, but the untimely death of a favourite son passed like a blight over his soul. Not a word escaped his lips in the way of complaint; but, *as if ill-used by God,* he never showed a cheerful countenance again. He gave way to sorrow, and soon his body was affected. He sunk into an apathetic state of mind, and his soul lost all relish for communion with God—till, wan, wasted, and refusing to be comforted, he pined away, and died.

2. If dealing with the unconverted, look up again to the Lord. Ply his arguments in the gospel, and do not soon desist. Remind them of his sovereignty and their sin. More especially, persist in drawing attention to the *gospel,* the good news, the tidings of bliss for the miserable. Persist in kindly calling attention to the satisfying, life-giving, grace of God in his Son. Thus Rom. 8:32, 'He that spared not his own Son, but delivered him up for us all, how shall he not

with him also freely give us all things?' Present this great truth again and again. It is the Spirit's wedge for splitting the cedar. Only receive *God's Son,* and *with him* you get all things. Only lift up that desponding eye and see the grace of *God's Son,* and *with him* you discover the remedy for your heart-breaking sorrow. Only believe this testimony, and welcome to your sad heart *God's Son,* who was so delivered up for us, and *with him* you find hope regarding all else lighting up your soul.

24

THE SORROW OF THE WORLD

1 Sam: 28:15. 'And Saul answered, I am sore distressed; for the Philistines make war against me, and God is departed from me, and answereth me no more, neither by prophets nor by dreams; therefore have I called thee, that thou mayest make known unto me what I shall do.'

> Compare 31:4. 'And Saul took a sword and fell upon it.' 1. This man gave way to his trouble, and never looked a forgiving God in the face; for sorrow weighed down his soul 2. He concluded there was *no way* of acceptance for him, because his own way was unsuccessful 3. He *supposed* God had finally forsaken his soul; but God had never said so. 4. He was the victim of wounded pride also; he seems to say, 'Let him strike, I am ready to suffer as he chooses.' 5. See the end—death, suicide. 6. God sees no excuse for Saul, for read verses 17-19.[1]

---

[1] 'Despair is hope stark dead, as presumption is hope stark mad.'—*Adams.* 'Despair makes men God's judge. It is a controller of the promises, a contradictor of Christ.'—*Bunyan.*

The Sorrow of the World

Gen. 4:13-14. 'My punishment is greater than I can bear. Behold, thou hast driven me out this day from the face of the earth.'

> 1. This man only grieved over his suffering. 2. He never sought God's love. 3. The clouds of sorrow hid from his view the sins which called for these sufferings. Beware!

Matt. 27:3, 5. 'Then Judas, which had betrayed him, when he saw that he was condemned, repented him . . . And he cast down the pieces of silver in the temple, and departed, and went and hanged himself.'

2 Cor. 7:10. 'The sorrow of the world worketh death.'

> 1. Sorrow for loss of friends, wealth, station, name, influence, place, may become this kind of sorrow, if the eye of the sorrowful looks only at the worldly side of the affliction. 2. To turn 'sorrow of the world' into 'godly sorrow', the sorrowful must, through his tears and with his heavy heart, look up to the Lord Jesus at the right hand of God, and lay the burden at his feet.'

2 Cor. 2:7. 'Lest perhaps such a one should be swallowed up with overmuch sorrow.'

> It is *'overmuch'*, if it put out of our heart not only all friends and earthly objects, but God, the Father of mercies. Should the broken cisterns make us forget the 'Fountain of living water'?

Prov. 12:25. 'Heaviness in the heart of a man maketh

it stoop. But a good word maketh it glad.'

> 1. So long as the 'good word' can make it glad again, the heart is not overmuch in sorrow. 2. So long as *God's* 'good word', the gospel of his Son, can gladden it, the heart is not under the power of the 'sorrow of the world'. 3. If, however, even God's good word give it no joy, the sorrowful has reason to fear lest he become like Cain, or Saul, or Ahithophel (2 *Sam.* 17:22), or Judas.

Prov. 17:22. 'A merry heart doeth good, like a medicine; but a broken spirit drieth the bones.'

> 1. There really is such a wasting disease as 'sorrow of the world', a 'broken spirit'. 2. There is a remedy for this disease, by which that broken spirit may become 'a merry heart'. 3. The cure is found, 2 Chron. 7:10, 'Merry in heart for the goodness that the Lord had shewn unto David, and to Solomon, and to Israel his people.' Think, O sorrowful one, on a sovereign God's sure mercies, promised then, fulfilled now; think of his beloved Son, in whom we have redemption, through his blood. There is 'joy and peace in believing'.

Job 6:10. 'Yea, I would harden myself in sorrow. Let him not spare; for I have not concealed the words of the Holy One.'

> 1. A believer may fall into 'sorrow of the world'. Here is an instance. 2. Job invites God to send sorer trouble still, that he may die. 3. He does so, in the belief that it would be better to depart than to live thus wretchedly, and expresses his hope in death by the clause, 'I have not concealed [or denied] the words of the Holy One'—I am his servant. But,

4. This is 'sorrow of the world';—for he is so sorrowful as to wish to die merely because of sorrow, not because it would be for God's glory, nor yet in order to be *holier*.

1 Kings 19:4-5. 'He came and sat down under a juniper tree: and he requested for himself that he might die; and said, It is enough: now, O Lord, take away my life; for I am not better than my fathers. And as he lay and slept under the juniper tree, behold then an angel touched him, and said unto him, Arise and eat.'

> Another case of a believer under 'sorrow of the world'. See, 1. Elijah has no respect here to aught but his own vexatious disappointment. 2. See how graciously the Lord turns Elijah's thoughts to his God; for the Lord sends his angel to deal kindly with him, 3. This is the remedy for 'sorrow of the world'. Behold the love of God worth living a whole eternity to know, and feel, and tell. 4. A sorrowful wish to die, arising from vexation or suffering, is the 'sorrow of the world'. It is not as Phil. 1:20-22, 24. 5. How nearly Elijah, by his sorrow, missed his glorious fiery chariot!

Rev. 16:9-11. 'And men were scorched with great heat, and blasphemed the name of God which had power over these plagues, and they repented not to give him glory. And they gnawed their tongues for pain, and blasphemed the God of heaven because of their pains and their sores, and repented not to give him glory.'[2]

---

[2] 'Adversity of itself', says one, 'is as little gracious as prosperity. Years of suffering did not fit Charles II, to reign, but were worse than wasted upon him.'

Here is 'the sorrow of the world working' death, most awfully! Whereas, 'Grace teaches us in the midst of life's greatest comforts to be willing to die, and in the midst of its greatest crosses to be willing to live.'

Isa. 8:20-22. 'To the law and to the testimony: if they speak not according to this word, it is because there is no light in them. And they shall pass through the land hardly bestead [beset with difficutlies] and hungry: and it shall come to pass, that, when they shall be hungry, they shall fret themselves, and curse their king and their God, and look upward. And they shall look unto the earth; and behold trouble and darkness, dimness of anguish; and they shall be driven to darkness.'

> 1. What an impenetrable gloom! 'Sorrow of the world, working death.' 2. All arising from forsaking 'the law and the testimony'. 3. A return to the law and testimony must be the cure. Listen to the good news of love to the guilty through the cross of Christ. *N.B.*—The *law* is the revealed will of God; what *he teaches us*.

Jer, 45:2-5. 'O Baruch, thou didst say, Woe is me now, for the Lord hath added grief to my sorrow. I fainted in my sighing, and I find no rest. Thus shalt thou say unto him; the Lord saith thus, Behold, that which I have built will I break down . . . But thy life will I give unto thee for a prey in all places whither thou goest.'

> 1. Here is sorrow cured, when just about to become 'sorrow

of the world'. 2. God's voice, drawing the sorrowing soul's thoughts to himself, is that which brings the cure.

Psa. 69:29. 'But I am poor and sorrowful. Let thy salvation, O God, set me up on high.'

Exod. 6:9. 'And Moses spake so unto the children of Israel: but they hearkened not unto Moses for anguish of heart and for cruel bondage.'

> 1. See to what 'sorrow of the world' leads. Israel would fain have remained in Egyptian bondage. 2. What must they have thought of this state of mind, when soon after they did lift their eye upward to the Lord, and, 'by faith kept the passover', and then marched out in triumphant joy? How nearly they had lost all by indulging 'sorrow of the world'.

2 Cor. 6:10. 'As sorrowful, yet always rejoicing.'

> A believer's sorrow may be to him what the waves of the sea are to the boat, helping it onward. His sorrows send him to Christ for joy. He lays his head on the bosom of the Man of Sorrows.

Isa. 35:10. 'And the ransomed of the Lord shall return and come to Zion with songs and everlasting joy upon their heads. [What a garland!] They shall obtain joy and gladness, and sorrow and sighing shall flee away.'

> 1. It is *'the ransomed'* who enjoy all these hopes. Use the *ransom,* and joy comes in, a foretaste of the joy that will be yours at Christ's coming. 2. The same is reiterated, chap. 51:11. 3. Look *forward,* therefore, as well as *up-*

ward, that your soul may be quite cured of 'the sorrow of the world'.

Isa. 53:3. 'Acquainted with grief.'

Think of Christ under this view. Here is one come to you who was 'exceeding sorrowful, even unto death'. He knows the bitterness of the saddest heart.

John 16:20. 'Your sorrow shall be turned into joy.'

By faith in his first coming, and hope in his second, sorrow is dislodged. Hearken, this is Christ's voice; here is the Physician with the balm: though you think your lot sunless, moonless, starless.'

John 15:11. 'These things have I spoken unto you, that my joy might remain in you, and that your joy might be full.'

1. Christ can give to the most sorrowful, joy unspeakable.
2. He gives it by making known to the soul what *he has done,* and by showing to the soul what *he is still.* These are 'the things spoken of'.

———

O Holy Ghost, the Guide into all the truth, the Glorifier of Jesus, the Comforter, the Spirit of truth, the Spirit of grace, the Spirit of Christ, the Promise of the Father, the Spirit of counsel and of might, of love, power, and a sound mind—breathe the breath of life!